SHORTCHANGED

Tanya S Osensky

shortchanged

HEIGHT DISCRIMINATION

AND STRATEGIES FOR SOCIAL CHANGE

*ForeEdge*

ForeEdge
An imprint of
University Press of New England
www.upne.com
© 2018 Tanya S Osensky
All rights reserved
Manufactured in the United States of America
Designed by Mindy Basinger Hill
Typeset in Calluna Pro

For permission to reproduce
any of the material
in this book, contact Permissions,
University Press of New England,
One Court Street, Suite 250,
Lebanon NH 03766;
or visit www.upne.com

Library of Congress Cataloging-in-Publication Data

*Names*: Osensky, Tanya S, author.
*Title*: Shortchanged: height discrimination and strategies for social
    change / Tanya S Osensky.
*Description*: Lebanon NH : ForeEdge, An imprint
    of University Press of New England, [2017] |
    Includes bibliographical references.
*Identifiers*: LCCN 2017026542 (print) | LCCN 2017033764 (ebook) |
    ISBN 9781512601442 (epub, mobi, & pdf) | ISBN 9781512601428
    (cloth) | ISBN 9781512601435 (pbk.)
*Subjects*: LCSH: Short people—United States. | Physical-appearance-
    based bias—United States.
*Classification*: LCC HM1091 (ebook) | LCC HM1091 .O74 2017 (print) |
    DDC 306.4/613—dc23
LC record available at https://lccn.loc.gov/2017026542

5   4   3   2   1

TO EVERYONE
WHO HAS
EVER BEEN
UNDERESTIMATED.

# CONTENTS

Acknowledgments   *ix*

1   HEIGHT MATTERS   *1*
Your Highness   *1*
Lies, Damn Lies, and Statistics   *11*
Vertical Challenges: Practical Issues Confronting Short People   *16*
Small Cruelties: How Heightism Affects Children   *18*
A Little Grown-Up: How Heightism Affects Adults   *23*
Cultural Ideal: Height Is Right   *28*
No Small Injustice   *45*

2    HEIGHT DISCRIMINATION AGAINST CHILDREN   *51*

How Tall Is Your Fetus?   *52*

Charting Growth   *55*

Abnormally Healthy   *60*

Growth Hormone Therapy   *64*

Ethical and Moral Shortcomings   *69*

High Risk of Tallness   *75*

High Cost of Tallness   *78*

Short Story   *79*

A Superior Specimen   *84*

Higher Values   *88*

3    SHORTCHANGED IN THE WORKPLACE   *94*

Glass Ceiling in a Skyscraper   *97*

A Sizable Wage Gap   *101*

Wage Gaps: Height versus Gender versus Race   *105*

Legal Limitations   *113*

Measuring Up   *120*

4    A LITTLE PERSPECTIVE   *132*

Slight Evolutionary Edge   *133*

Short Is Powerful   *135*

Some Uplifting Words   *136*

5    ALTIMATE CHANGE   *148*

Summing It All Up   *148*

Check Your Tall Privilege   *152*

Making a Grand Difference   *156*

Notes   *163*

# ACKNOWLEDGMENTS

FIRST, MANY THANKS to Phyllis Deutsch and the team at University Press of New England for supporting this project when no one else believed in it. I appreciate all your work in shaping this book. Without you, it never would have found its way to readers.

I also would like to thank my friends Pam, Terri, and Susan, who have tolerated me through the writing of the book, talked things over, provided comments, and never made me feel like writing a book about height discrimination was a ridiculous idea.

My deepest gratitude goes out to my wonderful husband Rick, who is the most thoughtful, compassionate, and loving person I have ever known. I am also grateful for and proud of our two amazing sons, Adam and Asher. My three guys are the love of my life. Together with my mother, who has always supported and encouraged me, my family has been my greatest inspiration.

I am sure there are many other people I could thank, but I am keeping these acknowledgments short and sweet . . . like me!

SHORTCHANGED

# height matters

Long or short,
a stick is always a stick;
tall or short,
people are always people.
CHINESE PROVERB

## YOUR HIGHNESS

Ask yourself: Would you like to be taller? Chances are, you probably would answer yes. Except for those who are already very tall, most people would not mind being a little taller than we are already. If scientists could figure out a painless, cheap, and easy way to add a few inches to our height, without any negative side effects, many people would gladly do it. Not only do many of us want to be taller than we already are, but when we are asked what our height is, we tend to "round up" an inch or two. It is generally accepted that people round up their height, even on official documents like driver's licenses.

Why is there this widespread desire to be taller, and why do we tend to embellish our height? We usually don't think about it, but we instinctively perceive tallness as a positive thing. We seem to have an intuition that being taller carries some advantage over being shorter. For most of us, it just feels better to say that we are a bit taller than we really are, as though tallness is worthy of more respect, as if having an extra inch or two is some sort of accomplishment. Without reflecting on the reasons for wanting to be taller or for claiming to be taller, we just know in our gut that taller is better.

Perhaps for those who are generally happy with their height, adding only a few inches would make no difference. Consider then, how much money would you be willing to accept to be under five foot tall (about 153 cm) for the rest of your life? This is a twist on a study by Ohio State University professor Philip Mazzocco et al.,[1] in which he asked white people how much money it would take for them to accept being black for the rest of their lives. Most people likely think that being a little bit short is no big deal. Those of us who are of average height or taller probably would not think twice about giving up an inch or two, because that would still be in the range of what is considered "normal" height. But when asked about being an outlier, at under five feet, we might really pause and think about it. We would likely sense that such a short frame would no longer be perceived as normal. It is as if we instinctively feel that being extremely short would mean having to give up a significant advantage.

If you would require a great deal of money to accept being under five feet tall for the rest of your life, then you realize that being tall is an advantage that has real value. What has been called "tall privilege" refers to the social deference that tall people receive in our society just because of their height, without their actually doing anything to deserve it. Taller stature comes with having greater influence in social relationships and leads to certain benefits in the workplace, such as more leadership opportunities, higher pay, and other advantages that are explored later in this book. This may not be very noticeable when considering those who are only slightly shorter than average, but it becomes obvious to those who are closer to the extreme end of the height curve. It also is very striking when we are facing a situation in which two individuals are being compared, because our perception of someone's height is relative. We intuitively understand that taller individuals are advantaged by this deference; otherwise we would not wish to be a little bit taller. As with male privilege and white privilege, those who are tall do not realize consciously that this privilege exists, but the fact that many people tend to round up their height and want to be taller speaks to our unconscious acknowledgment of this privilege.

We not only think positively of tallness in and of itself, but also we tend to think negatively about shortness. Those who benefit from the tall privilege have a sense of entitlement to its advantages because that is all they have known. Unfortunately, this sense of entitlement also comes with the corresponding sense of disdain that some taller people feel for those who are shorter. Short people, especially those on the tail end of the height spectrum, experience this disdain in several ways, from general social disrespect that leads to feelings of shame and inferiority to real workplace discrimination that affects income and career success.

Our society seems to be very comfortable with openly expressing disrespect toward short people. We seem to accept teasing and comments related to height in ways that would be considered rude if directed at those who are overweight or otherwise different from the norm. Usually the teasing is meant to be friendly, and the taller person does not mean any offense. However, most people would consider it impolite to comment about any other physical feature, such as weight or nose size, unless it was meant as a compliment. For example, we would never start a conversation by saying something like, "Wow, you have a large nose; have you ever considered a nose job?" or "Wow, you are so heavy; exactly how much do you weigh?" That would be considered rude. But no one thinks it is rude to joke and comment about a short person's unusual height in a similar manner: "Wow, you are so short; exactly how tall are you?"

It seems to be generally acceptable to make comments such as, "Wow, you are so short!" when we would never consider asking how much another person weighs or saying to an obese person, "Wow, you are so fat!" We would never point out to someone that he or she has a very large mole on his or her face, as though the owner of the mole had no idea. Yet it is socially accepted to point out the most obvious characteristic about a short person—his or her height—as though the short person were completely unaware of this particular attribute.

Many of us who are otherwise polite and sensitive about others' feelings still find it humorous to joke about or tease short people about their height. Telling a short person to stand up when the person is already standing is a common jibe. Other types of offenses are more subtle and indirect, including observations about how a person's fourth-grade son or daughter has already surpassed the person in height. Even people who are themselves relatively short relish an opportunity to be cruel when they meet someone who is even shorter, pointing out with glee how great it is to be standing next to him or her because the shorter individual makes them feel taller for a change. Aside from thoughtless jokes and comments, we feel comfortable directing a wide variety of behaviors at shorter individuals that we would not dare with taller individuals, such as patting them on the head, lifting them off the ground, frequently interrupting them while they speak, discounting their opinions and ideas as silly or irrelevant, and otherwise treating them like children. We so casually express our bias against short people that we do not even realize we are doing it. We rarely, if ever, give it any thought.

Despite the seemingly harmless intent behind such teasing and thoughtless behavior toward short people, most of us have not considered the fact that such disrespect is really intended to belittle and publicly humiliate them. Although social norms dictate that comments about an individual's physical traits are rude, we generally do not make that connection when it comes to height. Most of us would not consider ourselves to be prejudiced about someone based on a physical trait, but it does not occur to us that demeaning someone based on height—an inherent physical trait that cannot be changed or concealed—is really no different than demeaning someone based on any other inherent physical trait, such as race or gender. Unlike disrespect toward racial minorities or women, in our culture disrespect toward short people is widely accepted as perfectly normal. This is not to say that height discrimination is as severe or as harsh as racism or sexism, but rather to point out that height discrimination is just as commonplace, and that *unlike* racism and sexism, it is socially acceptable.

Of course everyone gets teased about something. As long as it is all good-natured fun and no harm is intended, what is the big deal? Perhaps rude incidents seem to be isolated and innocuous to those who are not themselves short. They appear to be trivial to those who do not experience them. Just as those who are not members of a racial minority often do not understand or even recognize incidents of racism, and just as men often do not recognize incidents of sexism, most people who are of average height or taller do not understand or recognize incidents that are disrespectful toward short people. In fact, this issue is so unacknowledged, even most short people themselves do not know there is a name for it: heightism.

Unfortunately, rude and thoughtless comments are just the tip of the iceberg when it comes to the way short people are commonly perceived and treated in our culture. Short people are frequently portrayed negatively in the media and are discriminated against at work. They endure more bullying in schools, in the social sphere, and in the workplace. Even seemingly rude but harmless conversations become grating when they occur repeatedly, especially in the workplace. It is particularly unnerving in the professional sphere, where the perception of authority and seriousness matters. Teasing comments and jokes about the height of a senior member of the management team in front of other coworkers and subordinates may be meant as jokes, but they are embarrassing. Whether intentional or not, such teasing belittles short people and lowers others' perceptions of them. When done in front of the person's subordinates, teasing about someone's physical characteristics undermines the short person's authority. The short person is forced to respond in kind so as not to appear unable to take a joke. The nature of the response is a catch-22: a weak response makes the person look even more humiliated and is likely to lead to even more ridicule, but a confrontation would negatively affect the person's work relationships and chances for advancing in the organization.

It is true that most people experience teasing in their lives about some physical attribute or another. The main difference between the regular teasing that many of us experience during childhood or adolescence and the disrespect that short people endure is that for short people, the teasing does not end after high school. It continues through adulthood, when most other adults no longer make fun of people for being fat or having overly large noses or protruding ears, at least in polite company.

Why do we seem inclined to put short people down? Like other biases, the height bias manifests subconsciously. We are inherently biased against individuals who are different from ourselves. We seem unable to help ourselves; our brains have been influenced through millions of years of evolution to classify all objects, animals, and other people into categories and hierarchies.[2] We automatically sort everything by weight, height, color, and shape, and we distinguish things by their differences. Similarly, the first thing we notice about people is their physical appearance: size, style, color, race, age, tone of voice, accent, and so forth. And then we assign preferences to these differences: some categories are considered superior, while others are judged to be inferior.[3] A difference in size is among the very first categories that we notice, the other two being color and gender.

It is not only that we are always aware of our own height in relation to others,' but our visual perception bias causes us to expect a positive relationship between an item's size and its corresponding worth or status.[4] In other words, we perceive more valuable things to be larger than less valuable things. For example, coins that are larger are perceived to be more valuable than smaller coins, regardless of the coin's actual monetary value.[5] Conversely, we tend to think of most small things and people as fragile, weak, and in need of our protection.

Sociologists have suggested that the importance of height has evolutionary origins, because larger males are more likely to win fights and to attain social dominance.[6] In other words, we have evolved to associate height with strength and power.[7] When meeting new people, our minds automatically evaluate the relative difference in height in a fraction of a second. This mental process may have evolved as a means to determine threats to personal safety. But even when our safety is not at risk, we use this same process to evaluate other people in order to assess the relative physical "stature"—or the social standing—of each person.[8]

Aside from the evolutionary theory, our association of height with power may be rooted in how we perceived the world when we were children.[9] Our earliest childhood memories are of being small and supported by our parents. Parents seem huge and all powerful; they control us in almost every way. As children, we are tiny in our environment, and everything else, such as all the furniture in our homes, is huge and hard to reach. Parents both protect us and at times punish us. To look us in the eye, they must either crouch down on their knees or lift us up in their arms. Even when we grow into adults, often surpassing our parents' height, we are frequently surprised when we realize how small our parents really are, because we have always seen them as tall in our mind's eye.

Regardless of whether the evolutionary explanation has any merit, the fact is that we do prejudge people based on size. When evaluating another person, whether friend or opponent, whether consciously or unconsciously, we judge the taller person to be stronger, more authoritative, and more powerful.[10] This is why monarchs insisted on being called "Your Highness" and preferred to be seen seated on a throne, so that their subjects would be forced to look up to them and perceive them as larger than life. This is why people wear high-heeled shoes to enhance their height. The taller the person, the more he or she is perceived to be dominant and superior. Because taller individuals are deemed to be above those who are shorter, they consequently tend to emerge as leaders and end up attaining higher social status due to their elevated dominance position.[11]

We all have various unconscious biases, but over time those biases can harden into stereotypes and prejudices. They become the lens through which we process information and make decisions about people. When we think of bias, we generally think of skin color, gender, nationality, and age, but our visual perception bias also includes aspects of size and affects all of us, in every situation, all the time, in ways that are both minor and serious. In our society tallness is glorified while shortness is ridiculed. Taller people (both men and women) are considered to be more beautiful and are held in higher esteem than shorter people. We are more likely to be convinced and persuaded by tall people, and in the workplace we are more likely to hire and promote them. After all, we "look up" to those who are tall and automatically attribute positive personality characteristics to them, while we ascribe negative traits to those we "look down on."

In fact, the English language includes hundreds of idioms related to size, most of which convey the judgment that bigger is better. Words used to describe taller people are much more flattering than words used to describe shorter ones. Consider how the words *short, small,* and *little* are usually used in a negative light or to point out some sort of disadvantage (e.g., coming up short, getting the short end of the stick or being shortchanged, being small-minded, drawing the short straw, feeling small, belittling or diminishing someone), whereas advantages or positive qualities tend to be described by the words *tall, big,* and *large* (e.g., standing tall, riding high, the bigger person, looking up to someone, making it big). Children are often urged to eat vegetables and drink milk so they can grow up to be *big* and *strong.* As teens, we are warned that bad habits like smoking and drinking will *stunt our growth* (as bad as smoking and drinking are for our health, neither has ever been proven to stunt growth, but the prospect of stunted growth is a powerful motivator). We *look up* to someone we admire. We *look down on* a criminal, and it would be undignified to *stoop down* to his or her level.

These subtle and not-so-subtle cues have great consequences for how short people are treated throughout their lives. We seem to have a third sense about how short people "should" act. The general preference seems to be for short people to remain invisible and obedient, as we expect children to do. Perhaps this is because short people are child-sized, so we have a tendency to treat short adults like children. The recent trend to refer to children as short people further adds to our perception that a short adult's status is equivalent to a child's. When a short person fails to act powerlessly and instead displays assertiveness, intelligence, and competence, it produces a feeling of incongruity. The feeling is usually not acknowledged; it is intuitive. We feel uncomfortable, confused, and even irritated. We sense that something is wrong, even if we cannot identify what it is.

When short people behave in a way that contradicts our expectations, we reflexively attempt to belittle them and minimize their influence, to force them to fit into our preconceived notions. We tend to react to such short people as we would to a challenge. Parental feelings are triggered toward shorter people, even though we may not consciously realize this. These feelings are manifested in our response, which is often to become frustrated and try to force them "back in their place." We attempt to push them down into a position of powerlessness by condescending to them and excluding them from conversations. If these tactics fail, we may stoop to teasing them, with increasing cruelty and hostility. The need to exert authority stems from the desire to retain control and power, to avoid allowing the short people to appear stronger or bigger. These thoughts, feelings, and actions take place at a subconscious level, without our knowing or understanding why. Women and minorities often encounter similar reactions when they fail to meet our social expectations of them.

Name-calling and jokes about shortness are unacceptable yet commonplace. Still, many people seem surprised if a short person becomes upset after just having been dismissed or belittled. Short people are supposed to laugh it off when they are put down and humiliated. We expect them to hide or deny their hurt feelings. If short people complain that they find such jokes offensive or disrespectful, they are told to "get over it" or asked "can't you take a joke?" Would anyone in polite society say "get over it" to someone complaining about racist or sexist jokes? Why do well-mannered people not tell women and racial minorities that no one said life was fair, so they should learn to deal with it? Why is such disrespect toward short people tolerated and accepted in our culture while disrespect against others is not? People who otherwise would never display such disregard toward the feelings of others with physical differences often are ignorant of their own prejudice about height.

Prejudice against short people is pervasive and ingrained in our culture. We instinctively prejudge short people in several ways. First, we assume that short people who fail to laugh at a joke made at their expense are defensive and oversensitive because they have an inferiority complex. Second, we assume that short people who act assertively are trying to overcompensate for their size because they have an inferiority complex. And third, when short people act timid and quiet, we assume that they do so because they have an inferiority complex. The assumption that short people have an inferiority complex is widespread. Short people are assumed to be either too weak and timid or too aggressive and controlling as a presumed means to counteract their lack of physical height. It is as if we hold short people responsible for stupidly choosing not to be tall. As with other biases, no one takes the time to logically evaluate whether these assumptions are true or valid. We think we have some insight into the short person's mind. Utter lack of knowledge of psychology does not stop us from feeling competent to assess a short person's psychosocial health and declare a mental health diagnosis that we are completely unqualified to make.

The fact that we have a height bias has developed into acceptance of treating short people with disrespect. We do not seem to consider that behaving either belligerently or timidly is a very natural human response to being disrespected. Whether a short person reacts to mistreatment with anger or by losing confidence, it is not because that person has an inferiority complex or is attempting to overcompensate for an inferiority complex, but because he or she is simply reacting to being insulted in the same way that any other human being would react. By assuming that short people have an inferiority complex, we fall prey to a bias that has no basis in fact. It is totally irrational. In effect, we are blaming the victim for having a predictable reaction to another person's intolerant behavior. Short people are not inherently angry or timid, and they are no more likely to have an inferiority complex than any other person. To the extent that we have any preconceived ideas about their character or psychology, such ideas are irrational and harmful. By continuing to wrongfully assume certain character traits or psychosis based on height, we not only remain ignorant in our own prejudice, but we also contribute to the persistence of the bias in our culture.

Short people experience this bias all of their lives, and it cannot help but affect them. We are faced with a vicious circle: our societal expectations of short people tend to become reflected in the expectations they have of themselves, which leads to undermining their confidence and success, which in turn reinforces the social bias.

## LIES, DAMN LIES, AND STATISTICS

How do we even know what we mean when we consider a person to be short? This judgment seems to be quite subjective in social interactions, but usually a difference of five inches or more really stands out. Height is relative, so even on a basketball team on which most of the players are over six foot five and some even exceed seven feet, an otherwise-average man of five foot ten would be considered extremely short. On the other hand, a man who was five foot ten might be considered extremely tall in the Philippines, where the average height for a male is five foot four.

Generally speaking, there is a range of heights that most people consider to be "normal," but this range may be different depending on the situation and context. Even a person of average stature may experience height discrimination from time to time, but most of the height prejudice in our society is directed at those considered to be "extremely" short. What do we mean by "extremely" short? Scientists have found a way of mathematically classifying really short people.

Statistically speaking, height falls into what is referred to as a normal distribution, or a bell curve, as illustrated in chart 1.

The mathematical principle referred to as Gaussian distribution is based on the observation that in any series of measurements, most of the numbers crowd around the middle, with a gradual distribution of outlying measurements, which is depicted on a chart as this bell-shaped curve. The middle of the bell is the mean measurement, and the deviation from the mean increases as the measurements move farther from the middle. When plotting the heights of many individuals in a large

CHART 1 Normal or Standard Distribution Curve

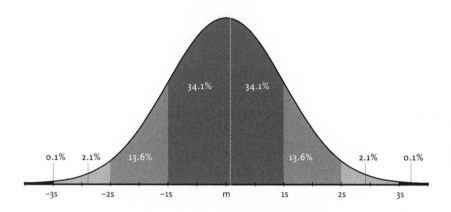

population, the variations in their heights form such a distribution, expressed as a percentile. For example, a person in the eightieth percentile would be shorter than 20 percent of all individuals in the population, and a person in the fifth percentile would be shorter than 95 percent of the population. This standard distribution of height is depicted whether one measures a population of students in a school, a population of employees in a company, or a population of citizens in a country.

Scientists also refer to these distributions as "standard deviation from the mean," or sigma ($\sigma$) units. Each standard deviation represents a fixed percentile. Zero is the fiftieth percentile (both the mean and median of the distribution). A very small number of measurements will fall outside the $-2\sigma$ to $+2\sigma$ range, which are considered to be extremes. In case of height, the median measurement would indicate the "average" height of a given population. Most people fall within about two-thirds of either side of this center, or within $2\sigma$, with each end trailing down toward the bottom axis of the chart, progressively diverging from the center. On the trailing ends of the statistical distribution are the extremes, representing about 4.4 percent of the population being measured (2.2 percent on each end), as shown in table 1.

When looking at the entire population of the United States, the lat-

TABLE 1

| "Short" End of the Chart | "Tall" End of the Chart |
| --- | --- |
| −3σ = 0.13th percentile | +3σ = 99.87th percentile |
| −2σ = 2.28th percentile | +2σ = 97.72nd percentile |
| −1σ = 15.87th percentile | +1σ = 84.13th percentile |

CHART 2  Height of Men and Women in the United States

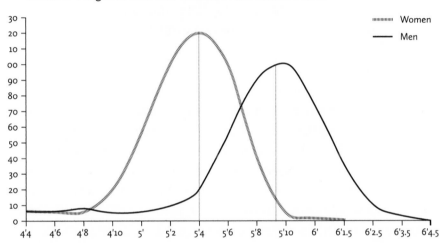

SOURCE: "Height in inches for females and males aged 20 and over: United States, 2007–2010." Anthropometric Reference Data for Children and Adults: United States, 2007–2010. Vital and Health Statistics, U.S. Department of Health and Human Services, Series 11, Number 252, October 2012.

est data available indicate that the average man is about 5'9.3" and the average woman is 5'3.8" tall.[12]

Chart 2 shows two distributions, one for men and one for women, each following the bell-curve shape of a statistical normal distribution. The curve demonstrates that while men are on average considerably taller than women, at around five foot seven the two curves overlap, showing that many women are as tall as many men. The curve also shows that a lot more people are on the shorter side of the curve than on the taller side, which implies that extremely short stature is much more common than extremely tall stature; that is, there are many more individuals of both genders in our population who would be considered extremely short than who would be considered extremely tall.

Based on the standard distribution principle, the two-thirds of either side of the average is the range of give or take two or three inches that is considered to be the "normal" range. Doctors typically consider height below the fifth percentile to be outside of the normal range for height. The most recent data collected by the National Center for Health Statistics indicate that men shorter than five foot four and women shorter than four foot eleven would fall outside of such a "normal range," which in the United States amounts to about sixteen million people. However, most people would consider those who fall into the bottom one-third of the distribution to be short (under about five foot seven for men and about five foot two for women, almost twenty-one million people).

Looking at height distribution data in isolation can be a bit misleading. In the United States, for example, the data from 2010 were collected from millions of people from a wide variety of ethnic and racial groups who were lumped together to make one beautiful chart. While a unifying picture of our population is appealing, a deeper review reveals that some racial and ethnic groups are taller and some are shorter. Black Americans are on average half an inch taller than whites, while Hispanic and Mexican Americans tend to be an inch or more shorter than whites. The same people who fall into the fifth percentile on the standard distribution curve would be considered within a "normal" range of height if they happened to be born into a Hispanic or Mexican American family or if they happen to live in many other countries of the world, including those in Latin America, Asia, and the Middle East. Even in some of the "first world" countries, such as Japan, Portugal, and Italy, the average heights are much shorter than those in the United States, so our society's bias toward specific heights is really focused on our particular culture. Those short people who are not within the "normal" range in our country's distribution curve would not be abnormal at all somewhere else. But what all cultures seem to agree on is that regardless of the average mean height in a particular population, those in the bottom 5 percent of it are extremely short.

As the standard distribution curve illustrates, there will always be people who will be considered extremely short. As a society continues to become statistically taller over time, the standard distribution curve shifts to the right, but the *percentage* of short people in the population overall does not change. In other words, over time the average or mean height in a population might increase from five foot ten to five foot eleven or even taller, but the percentage of people who would be considered extremely short or extremely tall will remain about 5 percent of the population. That is the nature of the standard distribution curve. There will therefore always be a substantial number of people in our society who will be considered extremely short. In fact, short stature is a matter of normal variation and part of the natural diversity of the human race. If we can stop considering these people abnormal and start treating them as normal and healthy members of the human race, then we can begin to work to eliminate the social inequities and prejudices that they face.

Interestingly, those individuals who fall above the ninety-fifth percentile are often quite proud of being tall, because our society views tallness as a superior trait. The individuals on the tall end of the spectrum find that their height helps them get ahead in life, love, business, and sports. They seem to occupy a commanding position and often appear to be powerful and imperious. In the past this has been less true for women who are extremely tall, but over the past few decades the prejudice against very tall women has largely disappeared, especially as women have made strides in the business world. Most likely this is because their height is comparable to men's. Regardless of gender, parents rarely complain that a child is too tall unless it is the result of an extremely rare medical condition. In practice, while the term *height discrimination* might be equally applicable to those who are either extremely short or extremely tall, there is not nearly as much social prejudice toward people who are extremely tall (aside from the annoyance of having to repeatedly answer the question "how's the weather up there?"). For this reason, this book's focus is on heightism toward people who are on the short side of the bell curve.

## VERTICAL CHALLENGES: PRACTICAL ISSUES CONFRONTING SHORT PEOPLE

Our perception of people's height is relative. Throughout our lives we always remain aware of our relative size in relation to others. At parties, in a crowded train or bus, in the elevator, in a movie line, and at concerts where everyone stands, we are forced to interact with other people in a way that makes height differences obvious. We unconsciously adjust our bodies to establish rapport with someone who is significantly taller or shorter and to make communication more comfortable. When there is a very noticeable height difference, just standing next to a person can be awkward. Shorter people must crane their necks to look up at taller people, causing neck aches and requiring individuals to step away from each other to make a conversation more comfortable. Taller people must look down to a much shorter person, often tending to slouch their backs or crouch down in an attempt to get closer to the shorter person's eye level. It is impossible to ignore a big difference in height.

Because many things we encounter in everyday life are designed for average-height individuals, those who are on either extreme of the height curve must deal with certain inconveniences. These include things like finding clothes and shoes that fit well and the fact that the average counter height in home kitchens and bathrooms may be uncomfortably high or low. While extremely tall people also encounter certain hardships that affect their day-to-day comfort (short stature is definitely an advantage when it comes to comfortably fitting into ever-narrower airplane seats), generally, tall stature is rewarded far more often than short stature. Many tables and chairs are designed so that a short person's feet dangle from the chair like a child's; when a chair can be lowered, the table is then uncomfortably high. This is usually not a big problem, but it could be quite humiliating in a boardroom meeting or an office executive conference room, where the perception of "executive presence" is a more valuable commodity than competence and intelligence.

Besides the practical, routine inconveniences that equally affect individuals who are both extremely tall and extremely short, being short can affect people's lives in ways that are far more serious. Product design issues are not only annoying and socially embarrassing, but sometimes can raise safety concerns. For example, car manufacturers apparently cannot profitably build a product that fits every driver, so they choose to focus on making a product that fits most people, leaving the shortest drivers with difficulty seeing well over the steering wheel or reaching the pedals. Although a short person is able to slide the driver's seat forward to reach better, being too close to the steering wheel is considered dangerous in the event of an accident, because the deployment of air bags, even when they are operating properly, can be too explosive for people at the short end of the height curve.

Most people know that air bags can hurt a child sitting in the front seat, and for this reason many people no longer permit children to sit in the front passenger seat. However, little attention is paid to how short adult drivers are affected by air bags. They are more likely to be seriously injured in relatively minor accidents by inflating air bags. A safety feature that was designed to protect a five-foot-ten, 165-pound male from injuries can be more dangerous to those under five foot four than not wearing a seatbelt in an accident.[13] Even a minor fender bender can cause the air bags to deploy, resulting in far greater injury to a short person than the minor cuts and bruises he or she otherwise would have sustained.

Given that the average woman in the United States is just under five foot four (in other words, a full 50 percent of all female drivers are under five foot four), one would think that there would be laws in place to provide better protection, or that the government would require a redesign of a feature intended to enhance safety so that it would provide the intended protection for short men and half of all female drivers. Car and air bag manufacturers advise that by sitting at least ten inches away from the steering wheel, the risk of injury from the air bag is reduced or even eliminated. However, they have not effectively communicated this advice, and it is obvious that most very short people must sit closer than that. Besides warnings to ensure that children should sit in the back seat, car manufacturers are not even required to warn drivers about this hazard, and it remains largely unknown.

## SMALL CRUELTIES:
## HOW HEIGHTISM AFFECTS CHILDREN

From the very earliest age, we learn that bigger size gets results. As early as toddlerhood, children who are bigger and stronger use their size and power to physically outmaneuver their smaller peers to get something they want. At this age, power struggles are typically decided by physical means, in a "natural selection" sort of way, such as hitting, biting, and kicking. Larger children tend to be more physically aggressive, because they learn that physical force yields positive results. The smaller children usually do not experience any negative psychological or social issues related to their short stature, because most preschool- and elementary-school-aged children have not yet learned to recognize on an intellectual level that there are differences in size. That realization usually comes as children get closer to middle school.

As children get older, they gradually learn from parental influence and socialization to curb and control their physical aggression most of the time. However, the aggression itself does not go away; it is simply redirected toward more verbal and psychological outlets. The teasing usually begins right before middle school age. Beginning around grades four or five and peaking during middle school, kids notice and focus on the physical differences between them. While biting and kicking decrease in frequency, slapping, pushing, whispering, and intimidation increase.

Children take cues from each other and copy the attitudes and prejudices that they see displayed by their families, classmates, and the media. At that age, kids (not just short kids, but all kids) begin to get teased and sometimes ostracized for their physical differences. Whether it be height, weight, a large nose, acne, braces, protruding ears, or for some other reason, some kids repeatedly are singled out. Short stature is not the only reason kids are bullied, but a noticeable difference in size makes someone an obvious target. Indeed, grown-ups unwittingly reinforce the bias by remarking about children's growth; comments such as "My, look how you've grown!" only emphasize the importance of size and can be damaging to a child who is not growing as fast as others.

The aggression and cruelty displayed by children can be stunning. During this period of life, appearance is the basis of how status is determined among children. Those who look like the societal ideal of beauty, height, and weight are usually the popular ones with the most social power. A hierarchy is formed, and those who differ from the norm receive as much deference and acceptance as their status permits. Differences in appearance are usually central to the focus. It is impossible to forget even for a moment who is bigger and who is smaller, who is going through a growth spurt, which girl is developing breasts early, which boy is displaying feminine attributes, and so forth. Those whose bodies differ from the norm even a little bit are teased. Those who differ from the norm by a lot tend to become the targets of intense and relentless humiliation and even torment. The targets are often made the subjects of cruel jokes, jeering, and hazing.

Short boys are more likely to be physically abused, because the taller kids cannot resist showing off their size and strength by grabbing, taunting, and pushing around those who are smaller. Common scenes in school hallways are spitting, "inadvertent" tripping, walking into people, and dumping their books out of their hands, forcing the victims to get down on their knees in shame to collect their belongings as the perpetrator walks away with a satisfied sneer. Such behaviors are raw displays of power. Boys may be appreciated as comic relief if they act like clowns, but they will be rejected and bullied if they attempt to resist the teasing.

This obsession with size, which seems to begin in early adolescence, becomes a central focus of our own identities. Bullies tend to pick on people smaller than themselves. Targets of bullying internalize the message that they are inferior and unwanted, which then becomes part of how they act. Children who are bullied sometimes develop low self-esteem if adults fail to intervene and help them learn good coping mechanisms or fail to provide appropriate emotional support. If bullying remains unaddressed, victims tend to grow into insecure and timid adults as their low self-esteem becomes permanently incorporated into how they perceive themselves. It becomes their very identity.

Bullying tends to have lasting effects that are difficult to forget or to overcome. Some victims develop tendencies to be shy and unassertive and to minimize their accomplishments. Those who were on the extreme ends of the height spectrum—both short and tall—experience loneliness, difficulty making friends, and sometimes intense angst. Even long after they have grown up and have become successful, adults who were very short or very tall as adolescents retain many painful memories about the bullying they experienced in their childhood and adolescence. They may not be thinking of these incidents in their daily lives, but when they are asked about them, these memories flood back to the surface, carrying the same emotional soreness as though time had stood still. Even when the teasing is merely occasional or minor, it seems to endure in memories that last long into adulthood. Those children who are teased for their height when young but later experience a growth spurt and eventually grow to normal adult height, or even become on the tall side, nevertheless remain burdened by their early experiences. This is why some people who are tall are perceived as shorter than they are. They cannot seem to shake the victim mentality that they experienced as children and thus continue to "act" short.

Children who are short are the victims of disrespect from well-meaning adults as well. Adults frequently treat children based on how old they look, rather than their chronological age. This can be a problem for kids who are very tall also, because adults expect them to be older than they really are. But for short children, being treated as if they're younger than they are can feel even more hurtful than the teasing they get from other kids.

Austin A. (not his real name) is a perfect example of how this plays out in real life. He was born in the fiftieth percentile in both length and weight, but over the first couple of years of his life his growth pattern shifted so that his height eventually became in the less than third percentile, and he has continued growing along that percentile. Needless to say, his parents were quite concerned about his growth trajectory and took him to several pediatric endocrinologists to try to determine the cause of his short stature. In the end, however, it was determined that his short stature was not due to any medical issue but was just genetic. Despite the apparent lack of growth, he was simply growing at his own consistent rate and was perfectly healthy and normal.

Austin has always been smart, funny, athletic and, during childhood, very confident. He was always the shortest kid in his class by far, at least a full head shorter than his peers, but until age eight or nine he did not display any negative behaviors that could have been attributed to his height. He did not even really notice that he was much shorter than other kids, or at least it never seemed to bother him. He was very active in tae kwon do and even reached black belt level when he was ten years old.

Around the time he was in fifth or sixth grade, however, he began to experience more teasing in school. He became increasingly sullen and withdrawn, but his parents attributed these changes to early teen behavior. By the time he was in seventh grade, he was beginning to show signs of depression. It became more severe after his family moved to a new neighborhood and he started going to a new school. He had a very difficult time adjusting to the new school and making friends. He felt out of place, as though he did not belong. His grades plummeted, and he never volunteered to speak up in class. He did not socialize and did not feel like playing sports. He quit tae kwon do. He was an easy target for teasing because he was different, and as a result, he lost much of his confidence. Whereas before he was outgoing and opinionated, he became timid and quiet. He even contemplated suicide.

After he started high school, the teasing subsided. Thanks to some counseling, Austin began to see things from a better perspective. By the time he was in tenth grade, he was four foot ten, still extremely short, but he had acquired many friends, both in and out of school, participated in team sports, and was active in his community. He was no longer timid and quiet, was not afraid to voice his opinions, and felt comfortable speaking up in class. He finally managed to adjust to the other kids' thoughtless comments. Although he is still ridiculed from time to time, he does not let it get to him because he has a close group of friends who treat him well, which has made a big difference in his ability to deal with ignorant comments from others.

However, Austin still encounters as much or more rudeness from adults as from other kids. Restaurant servers still often bring him the kids' menu and a kids' cup with a lid. He recalls a visit to a new doctor's office when he was twelve. The receptionist asked him his age, and when he responded she replied, "Are you sure? You look like you might be nine or ten. I have a twelve-year-old boy, and he is about half a foot taller than you." Another time, when he had just started high school, he was walking down the hallway and met up with the janitor. The janitor asked him what he was doing there because he looked too young and small to belong in the school. When he told the janitor that he was in ninth grade, the man acted surprised and commented that he sure did not look that age. There have been more than a few similar situations in which adults, who should know better, have uttered insensitive comments that have deeply hurt his feelings. They are especially hurtful coming from an adult in a medical office or school, who should be trained to be more sensitive to children's differences.

The point is that even when children and adolescents learn to manage and overcome teasing from their peers, heightism is a prejudice that pervades our society and attacks short people from all directions. While all kids get teased about something, teasing related to height does not happen just among children. Short children and teens experience disrespect not only from other children, but also from adults, even those in positions of authority, such as a nurse, teacher, or principal. It is even more difficult for children or teens to handle disrespect when it comes from out of left field from someone who is supposed to be there to support and protect them. We really cannot expect short children to have the wherewithal to stand up to thoughtless comments from adults; it should be our cultural and social expectation of all adults to be more conscious that this bias exists and to intentionally refrain from exhibiting it. It should never be acceptable for adults who interact with children as part of their jobs to treat children in a way that is offensive and disrespectful, particularly based on a physical trait.

A LITTLE GROWN-UP:

HOW HEIGHTISM AFFECTS ADULTS

Size tends to remain a persistent source of distress well into adulthood for many of us. In a society in which everything reminds a short person of just how short he or she is, it is not surprising that a social and cultural stigma has become associated with short stature. Our height perception bias plays out in the subtle power struggles in interpersonal relationships between friends and love partners. People seem to be programmed to keep physical size in the spotlight. Size-related power struggles continue even after we get older and have stopped growing.

An adult's relative height should be considered a childish concern, and we do not give it any thought. We want everyone to deny that the problem even exists. Unconsciously we want to believe that height should not make a difference in our interactions, so we assume it does not. However, height always affects our interactions. We are always keenly aware of others' relative height. Our glorification of the tall and the derision directed at short people have real social and material consequences. In the workplace, tall people automatically command power and respect until their behavior proves they don't deserve it, whereas short people are initially looked down upon and not taken seriously until they have demonstrated far greater talent, intelligence, and competence than their taller colleagues. They are paid less than tall people. They are regularly passed over for job opportunities and promotions.

Short men's struggles in this regard are more obvious than short women's. It is usually the tallest man who seems to have an advantage in groups of men. This effect is most apparent in sports and in the workplace. Men on a team tend to form a social hierarchy, dominated by the highest ranking "alpha" male, who is often the tallest and strongest male of the group. The hierarchy is frequently reinforced through belittling and indirect bullying among the smaller members of the group, each retaliating against the others with punches to the arm, pushes, verbal razzing, and aggressive horseplay that eventually filters down to the smallest victim. Each of the smaller members looks up to the alpha male and strives for his approval and praise. When describing a short man, the word *little* is prominent; he is usually labeled as a funny little man or, if he is assertive, as a determined little man. If he is disliked, he might be labeled as an annoying little man.

Of course there are many examples of short men who do achieve great career success, but it seems we are prone to put them down then, too. When a tall man achieves great success through aggressive ambition, it is attributed to his leadership ability, talent, intellect, and hard work. He is admired for being determined and bold. In contrast, when a short man achieves great success through aggressive ambition, he is often derided as Napoleonic or the "whiny little" boss. The reference to Napoleon is a derogatory description of an individual who is overcompensating for his shortcomings as a result of an inferiority complex. The term is used to belittle a short man by describing him as a belligerent tyrant seeking to cover up a physical deficiency. It is an insidious and hurtful stereotype.

In romantic relationships, a man's short stature, at least at the outset, is a significant disadvantage that must be overcome. It seems to be a general preference on the part of both men and women that the male should be taller than the female. Many women still consider short men undesirable as potential mates regardless of their other attributes, wealth, or social status. Women often do not wish to date them. A *20/20* story that aired on television on October 26, 2011, highlighted how short men are discriminated against in dating. The women on the program were asked whether they would date the men in a lineup that included some very short men, and the women actually said that the only way they would date a short man is if the other men in the lineup were murderers or child molesters.

Although things are slowly changing, much of the socialization of young girls still involves the fairy-tale ideal of being swept away by a tall and handsome Prince Charming, getting married, and living happily ever after. The vision of this Prince Charming does not usually involve a short man, no matter how well-built his body or how handsome his facial features. The phrase "short and handsome" sounds incongruous. Certainly a short man is likely to find that he has fewer potential mates to choose from than a taller man. This is a sad state of affairs, and it is the women who miss out on potentially meeting their "Mr. Right" when they arbitrarily judge men by their height. Yet short men tend to marry and have happy marriages, so the situation is not as dire as it appears at first blush. Perhaps women eventually realize that their initial assumptions about short men have been overly simplistic, or they first become friends with a short man and subsequently fall in love after getting to know him.

Of course women do not choose a man solely based on height, but the preference is evident across most, if not all, human cultures.[14] Because males are generally taller than females, it has become accepted that men *should* be large and strong while women *should* be diminutive and weak. These traits have become embedded as our defined ideal of beauty. We are accustomed to seeing a grown man who is taller and stronger than his female partner. Over time, these ideals have turned into stereotypes, and those who fail to live up to them have become stigmatized. What is really at issue is the relative power of the partners. Men prefer shorter women because they want to feel dominant and superior. Women echo the same preferences when they feel that a shorter man is somehow inferior and they would feel uncomfortable dominating him.

When a couple is made up of a taller woman with a shorter man, it is a novelty and a source of endless fascination. People assume that the woman is the dominant partner in the relationship. The smaller man is a stand-in for a child, who gets mothered by the woman. Once again, we tend to equate the man's smaller size with childhood and assume that he is immature. A couple whom others perceive as mismatched must be aware that dealing with insults will be a constant feature in their relationship. Even Tom Cruise, one of the most physically attractive and wealthy movie stars in the world, has been the focus of much attention in the media for dating and marrying women taller than he is.

Height discrimination may be more obvious when it happens to short men, but it is not exclusive to short men. Heightism colors our view of women, too. Most people believe that petite women have it made—that there are no negative repercussions for short women, because they fit into our cultural ideal (petite is how women are supposed to be). Short women are deemed to be the beneficiaries of positive attention because people tend to have a protective instinct toward them. In truth, however, being a short woman carries real, negative consequences, albeit sometimes more subtle than those faced by short men. We make certain instant judgments about short women's personalities and character, just as we do about short men. We generally consider shorter women to be more nurturing and motherly but also less intelligent, independent, and affluent than taller women.

Short women are expected to be submissive and are more likely to be perceived as unintelligent than taller women. As children, short girls tend to receive more attention from adults because they are doll-like and adorable. This does not end when the short girl remains small into adulthood. Society's expectations of a short woman are similar to those we have of a child: to be obedient, quiet, and unquestioning of the authority of the taller and more powerful. Since she is not as tall as an adult, the woman is expected to act as a child; indeed, short women are frequently mistaken for children. As long as she conforms to these expectations, the short woman will be accepted. Women who conform to this stereotype and do not mind being treated as children often do benefit from a great deal of attention and approval from others, particularly from men. Tall men have a hard time resisting the urge to pick up a short woman, like a child or a doll. It is not uncommon for a short woman to be called "a little girl" by complete strangers and friends alike, without their realizing they are being rude.

The attention may feel good initially, but it is degrading. While men (and taller women) unconsciously may experience an urge to be protective toward short women, they frequently take this to the point of being overprotective. In fact, the protective urge toward another adult is patronizing and disrespectful, because grown women are adults. Adults usually do not wish to be treated as children and should be perfectly capable of protecting themselves. If the woman has intelligence and ambitious goals for a professional career, treating her like a child or even making the assumption that she is young and naïve is condescending. In a professional environment it is utterly demeaning to treat a colleague as a child, to pat her on the head, or to lift her off the ground. These actions make the woman feel childlike and inconsequential, whether that is the intention or not.

Often short women do not find their height to be a problem in life until they encounter workplace discrimination in a way that makes them realize that they will have a harder time attaining professional success than taller women. While many short women (as well as men) have certainly achieved impressive careers, they have had to overcome greater obstacles to get to those higher levels. Short professional women, such as lawyers, doctors, accountants, professors, executives, and elected officials, often find it especially challenging to be taken seriously. People expect an expert to look distinguished (and often male, balding or graying, and older). To be successful in such professions, perceptions are critical, and one must have the appearance of having authority and influence. Taller women find it easier to achieve professional success; they are perceived to be more intelligent, affluent, assertive, and ambitious than shorter women.[15]

In my own career as an attorney, and after speaking with other short professional women, I have come to the conclusion that short women typically are viewed as lacking the gravitas to reach the very top of the professional ladder. While there may be some notable exceptions, such as Madeleine Albright (four foot ten) and Ruth Westheimer (four foot seven), as a general rule, short women are less likely to achieve the top of the career ladder than women who are taller than average. There are far fewer very short individuals in the professions than in other fields. Short women are much more likely to achieve success in creative endeavors such as acting, music, and art than in business, politics, the professions, or academia. Perhaps this is because we tend to assume that a short woman is younger than her years, and that therefore it is impossible for her to have as much expertise and experience as she does. We tend to assume that a taller person's opinions and knowledge are more credible. No matter how accomplished and knowledgeable she is professionally, instead of being able to rely on her track record, a short woman has to prove herself at each and every encounter before she is taken seriously as a voice of authority. Even Madeleine Albright and Ruth Westheimer were virtually unknown until relatively late in life, when they already looked as "wise" as they were.

Many years ago, before women were free to pursue professional careers, being petite was considered the female ideal. For those women who appreciate being admired for their looks, being short is not an obstacle. In today's business world, however, tall women are all the fashion. Tall women are idealized and are more respected in academic and professional pursuits. At work, short stature is an obstacle, regardless of gender. "You're so cute" may be an appropriate thing to say in a romantic context, but it is not a remark that shows respect in a professional setting. In a world where taller is better, smaller women are looked down upon both for being women and for being short. Where tall women are encouraged to feel powerful and valued, short women are encouraged to act inferior and weak. Attaining professional success is difficult. Being a woman makes it more difficult; being a short woman makes it extremely difficult.


## CULTURAL IDEAL: HEIGHT IS RIGHT

The evidence of stigma against short people is most prevalent and visible in our popular culture. Many television shows and movies have portrayed short characters in a negative light. The stigma even surfaces in music, such as the irritating "Short People" song by Randy Newman, which has been used as a means to bully short people since 1977. The song's lyrics, which include such refrains as "short people got no reason to live" and "I don't want no short people 'round here" are a prejudiced attack on short people, articulating the societal bias and putting into words those hidden feelings that short people should just disappear from existence and become invisible. Even though Newman himself claimed that the song is about prejudice, written from the point of view of a biased person, that subtlety was lost on most listeners, who easily misunderstood the words as reflecting Newman's own perspective. The fact that Randy Newman's greatest hits albums all include the song has helped it to endure. The song's popularity has waned, but regrettably it still has not completely disappeared from the media, and one can still find relatively recent videos of it on YouTube and modern recordings of it on other Web sites.

It should not surprise anyone that the media celebrate the tall and thin. In movies and on television, short people are commonly portrayed in nonleading or supporting roles. Both women and men who are tall and thin are most often considered attractive targets worthy of romantic pursuit. Short characters in television shows and movies usually are relegated to the role of the taller character's friend or sidekick, such as Tonto to the Lone Ranger, Barney Rubble to Fred Flintstone, Robin to Batman, and George Costanza to Jerry Seinfeld. This has been a trend for both male and female characters; just as Hercules's shorter sidekick was Iolaus, Xena's shorter sidekick was Gabrielle. Short female actresses are most often cast in the role of the friend to a taller character, such as Nicole Richie as Paris Hilton's friend in *The Simple Life,* Rory's friend Lane on the *Gilmore Girls,* and Sarah Jessica Parker as Lori Singer's friend in the movie *Footloose.* The few powerful female characters in movies and television shows have mostly been much taller than average: for example, Gina Torres's character Jessica Pearson in *Suits,* Jane Fonda's character Leona Lansing in *Newsroom,* Christine Baranski's character Diana Lockhart in *The Good Wife,* Robin Wright's character Claire Underwood in *House of Cards,* and Emily Deschanel's character Temperance Brennan in *Bones.* The few exceptions to this general rule include Emilia Clarke's portrayal of Daenerys Targaryen in *Game of Thrones* and Linda Hunt's character Henrietta Lange in *NCIS: Los Angeles.*

It is rare for short male characters to be represented as strong and powerful in television and movies, or even with dignity. A few notable exceptions that depict short characters as intelligent and successful are Michael J. Fox's role in *Spin City,* Peter Dinklage's role as Tyrion in

*Game of Thrones,* and Johnny Galecki and Simon Helfberg's roles in the *Big Bang Theory.* Far more common are depictions of short characters as inconsequential or merely supportive of taller characters, or worse, in a way that is disrespectful. More often short men serve as the comic relief—they either act as foolish sidekicks (Don Knotts as Barney Fife on the *Andy Griffith Show,* George Costanza on *Seinfeld,* and Carlton Banks on *Fresh Prince of Bel Air*); angry, vulgar sleazebags (Danny DeVito as Louie in *Taxi* and David Spade as Russell Dunbar in *Rules of Engagement*); or pathetic losers (Danny DeVito as Vincent Benedict in the movie *Twins*). The recurring message in the media is both overtly and covertly anti-short. Short men are particularly targeted as the subjects of insulting jokes and negative stereotypes on television shows and in movies. Some characters, such as George Costanza of *Seinfeld* and Russell Dunbar of *Rules of Engagement,* are portrayed as merely clownish and ineffective, while occasionally there is a character, such as Han Lee in *Two Broke Girls,* who is relentlessly mocked for his height in almost every episode. Even when intended to be humorous, these types of representations encourage hostility toward short people by portraying the intimidation of short people as commonplace and acceptable, which suggests that it is okay to dismiss and belittle them.

Apparently heightism remains alive and well on the Final Frontier; even in the egalitarian future world of *Star Trek,* where all other forms of discrimination have been overcome, short characters and species are mocked and portrayed as inferior. The Ferengi race has been depicted as short, repulsive, and misogynistic characters who cannot be trusted. While many critics have claimed that the Ferengi represent negative Jewish stereotypes, the link to heightism is also worth exploring. Besides smaller species, no other types of species envisioned by this future *Star Trek* universe have been regarded with complete disdain and ridicule. For example, the movie *Star Trek Beyond* (2016) begins with a scene in which Captain Kirk is entreating a ferocious-looking race to accept a token of peace from its enemy. The race appears to be scary and vicious, glaring down at him. They do not believe his claim that this token is a peace offering, arguing that it is stolen (which later turns out to be true). When he is unable to convince them, they get angry and start attacking him, and it becomes clear that despite their initial ferocious appearance, they are actually very small creatures. They descend on him like a school of piranhas, biting and swarming around him as he does his best to swat them away, looking merely annoyed. When he is beamed back to his ship and is asked whether his mission was successful, he responds, "No, I came up . . . short." Kirk's interaction with this species is never mentioned again, and their role in the movie is clearly limited to the sole purpose of serving as comic relief; otherwise, the species is completely irrelevant to the plot. As if this were not bad enough, Kirk is later shown joking about another small creature, who is depicted as not wearing any pants. Again, no other character of any race or species in this diverse and tolerant world is ever depicted as frivolous jesters due to their physical characteristics.

Although the negative messages in the media are most often about short men, women have not been ignored. Donald Trump is well known for his degrading comments about women generally, but in a 2005 interview with Howard Stern he vulgarly remarked about the actress Eva Longoria's short stature: "She's really cute, I have to tell you. . . . She's about five foot one. Do you like girls that are five foot one? They come up to you know where. She's very, very short." Likewise, in August 2015 on her talk show, host Wendy Williams put down singer Ariana Grande's appearance: "She's 21. She'll forever look 12." The audience laughed, as Williams continued: "Which, I don't mean that in a good way. . . . You know, it's nice to look younger than you are, but when you look too young, and then you're short—she's only like four foot eleven. I don't look at her as, like, a woman." Williams's comments reveal the stereotypical view that short women are equivalent to children. While the outspoken Ms. Williams frequently rants about celebrities, this body-shaming tirade was particularly directed at Ariana Grande's inherent physical trait. Had Ms. Williams ever made similar comments about another person's skin color or any other physical characteristic, her show might have been canceled immediately. Even though Ariana's fans banded together to try to get the show canceled, they were unsuccessful. When Wendy Williams was asked whether Grande's fans were being overly sensitive (a common response to people complaining of height discrimination), her reply was that "they're kids," again equating the issue of height discrimination with a childish concern.

Even movies for children often portray short characters negatively. For example, in *Shrek* (2001) the depiction of the short and evil tyrant Farquaad is an obvious reference to the stereotypical assumption that short men have an inferiority complex, because he is repeatedly shown in situations in which he is comically trying to overcompensate for his lack of height. In one scene there is a joke about the size of his castle, and Shrek says to the donkey: "Do you think maybe he's compensating for something?" Even the character's name is a subtle reference to the word *fuckwad* to underline his standing as a complete loser. The overall message sent to kids is that it is better for Princess Fiona to marry an ugly ogre rather than a short man.

The recent Disney movie *Zootopia* (2016), which purports to be about how discrimination is wrong, sends kids an awkward message that it is difficult to overcome the stereotype that smaller creatures are weak, so we should just be patient. Bunny Hops is a rabbit who is told that she is too small to be a police officer, but she is determined and makes it through training anyway. Her first assignment is viewed as the easiest and most harmless job a small, incompetent creature like her could perform: meter maid. Despite this initial assignment, she ends up partnering with a fox who helps her investigate a mystery and solve a "serious" crime. Throughout the movie, stereotypes of all kinds abound, and the big message seems to be that those who are the victims of discrimination should just quietly endure it. While most critics interpreted this movie as being solely about racial stereotypes, particularly involving the predator animals, its observations about Bunny Hops are more applicable to height discrimination, and this aspect of the movie has been largely ignored by critics. The message about believing in yourself is a great one, but it completely misses the point by failing to acknowledge or explain why Bunny should patiently endure heightism toward herself while bravely confronting her own racial prejudice and learning tolerance toward victims of racism.

Hollywood movies and TV shows for adults have portrayed blatant heightism as a normal state of affairs, which has served to reinforce stereotypes against short people. *Captain America: The First Avenger* (2011) is one of the worst examples of a movie that screams that taller is better, repeatedly depicting the main character as a pathetic and sickly weakling of five foot four before he becomes Captain America and as a tall and powerful hero after he takes drugs to reach his Captain America height of six foot two. Aside from the terrible message to teenage boys that they should take drugs to become taller and stronger, the movie repeatedly makes the point that short men are weak and pitiful losers, and that they can't be heroes. They also can't have a girlfriend: Captain's love interest in the movie felt sorry for him when he was five foot four but fell in love with him after he became six foot two.

Many Hollywood movies include a scene or two that feature heightist dialogue or interaction presented as so casual and ordinary that no one gives it a second thought. For example, in the beginning of *American Sniper* (2014) the leading lady is approached by a man at a bar who looks about average height. When he offers to buy her a drink, she rejects him, asking, "Will a drink make you six inches taller and charming?" She is then approached by Bradley Cooper's six-foot-one character, who asks, "Am I tall enough to buy you a drink?"

Similarly, in the HBO show *The Newsroom* (2012–2014), while Jeff Daniels's character Will McAvoy is in jail for contempt of court, he is confronted and threatened by his cell mate. Will's immediate response is to jump up and command his cell mate to stand up. When the man stands up, Will gets right up to his face and says: "I want you to see that I have four inches on you. . . ." Will then threatens physical reprisal if his cell mate does not back down. Of course his cell mate immediately backs down. The scene's dialogue and Will's reaction to a shorter man's threatening behavior represent the idea that being taller is the only qualification needed to control and overpower someone, that height makes right, and that shorter people should quietly accept their inferior place and step aside to let the taller people lead. The incongruous feature between this scene and the rest of this show is that Will's character is otherwise represented as someone who considers prejudice to be wrong. The scene stands out in stark contrast because of the casual and routine way that he uses his tallness against another person. What was most noticeable about this scene is how unnoticeable it was.

One notable Hollywood product that attempts to address the issue of height discrimination in a serious way is the 2003 movie *The Station Agent.* Peter Dinklage stars as a man with dwarfism who seeks solitude in an abandoned train station, trying to get away from the daily cruelty he experiences based on his height. Even though he is handsome, the only sexual interest he receives is from someone who wants to satisfy her curiosity about his body. Gradually he allows two other lonely souls to become his friends. The movie depicts a sad, lonely perspective on the characters' lives, focusing more on their fears and anger, and it never reaches any sort of resolution. Dinklage strikes the perfect tone as a short person who feels rage about the way people treat him but nevertheless manages to act with great dignity for as long as possible. While at a bar one evening, he notices the other patrons staring and laughing at him, and he finally gets angry because he can no longer take being treated as a circus freak. He stands up on his chair and yells, "Here I am! Take a look," and then slumps back down in his chair. *The Station Agent* is the one and only movie that addresses the point of view that there are far too many people in this world who treat short people with disrespect and that it causes short people to endure great pain and suffering.

Unlike many other short actors, Dinklage has made it a point to ensure that the roles he plays do not cast him in a ridiculous light. He told the *New York Times Magazine* in 2012 that from the beginning of his career, he refused to play elves or leprechauns, even though such jobs would have helped him advance as an actor before he became well-known, because he did not want to perpetuate the exploitation that often happens to dwarf actors.[16] Dinklage's insistence on selecting roles that are complex and intelligent, and his performances in movies and shows such as *The Station Agent* and *Game of Thrones,* should send a strong message to other short actors that it is not necessary to perform the part of the buffoon or to accept relentless body shaming in order to find success as a short actor in Hollywood. Some may think that because Dinklage is himself a dwarf, his physical disability inspires a certain seriousness in the audience that may not be granted to actors who are short but who do not have dwarfism. But that assumption is without merit, because many other short actors also have never stooped to acting the role of a clown in a way that only serves to reinforce social stereotypes about short men, including Michael J. Fox, Dustin Hoffman, Elijah Wood, and Al Pacino.

In contrast, the actor Mathew Moy, who stars as the short Korean immigrant Han Lee in the CBS show *Two Broke Girls,* is one of many Hollywood actors who seem eager to play into the stereotype, much to their own humiliation. Often described by the media as "diminutive," the five-foot-one actor has been criticized for playing into negative racial stereotypes, speaking broken English (even though he is a native English speaker) and enduring many racist jokes. But as part of this show, his character is also regularly the butt of insipid and unrelenting short jokes, which has received no attention in the media. In fact, media reported favorably that the show responded to criticism about racist jokes by toning those down and replacing them with jokes about Han Lee's height. Moy is proud of his success and has bragged about having been made fun of all his life. However, despite his financial success as a Hollywood actor, he has complained publicly about having trouble getting involved romantically with someone who is interested in him for reasons besides his fame. Perhaps if short actors like Moy refused to participate in their own public humiliation and instead spoke out against heightism, his experience might be different. As Peter Dinklage remarked in the *New York Times Magazine* interview previously cited, "You can say no. You can *not* be the object of ridicule."[17]

Outside of the United States, the issue of heightism has been the subject of several popular movies, most notably *Corazon de Leon* (*Lionheart*), a 2013 Argentinian box-office hit romantic comedy. In the movie, Ivana is a beautiful female lawyer who loses her cell phone and receives a call from Leon, who has found the phone and would like to return it. During their phone conversation, the two establish a rapport and decide to meet so that Leon can return Ivana's phone. At the meeting, however, Ivana discovers that although she has a lot in common with the charismatic and confident Leon, he is only about four foot five. Despite her having been charmed on the phone, the only thing that helps to overcome Ivana's initial revulsion about his height is the fact that he is fabulously wealthy and takes her parachuting out of his private plane on their first date. Fortunately the fact of Leon's wealth is minimized somewhat during the rest of the movie, and it is made clear that Ivana falls in love with him for his character and personality rather than his wallet. However, the fact remains that initially the only way their relationship could progress to the next step was due to his enormous wealth. The rest of the movie is about Ivana's attempts to overcome her prejudice about his height (despite his great wealth).

The actor playing Leon is Guillermo Campanella, a popular Argentinian actor and comedian who has enjoyed a long and successful career. Although he is five foot seven, his height was digitally reduced to four foot five for the movie to accentuate the height difference between the actors. Throughout the movie, Ivana struggles with her inability to reconcile her love and respect for the man, who is perfect in every other way, being intelligent, kind, and funny, with the prejudice relentlessly displayed by society toward his height. But his determination to be with her and his charming personality eventually win her over.

Although Mr. Campanella's acting is excellent, it is unclear why the director elected to have his height digitally modified rather than use a real dwarf actor for the role. The idea that his height had to be digitally modified to make a point suggests that the filmmakers believed that heightism is only an issue for those who have dwarfism. While it is true that dwarfs experience severe heightism, it would have been much more realistic and interesting to explore this social prejudice if Ivana's love interest had been only a few inches shorter than she (as is much more likely in real life), because absent dwarfism, some women still care too much about other people's perceptions and expectations, even if it means losing out on the perfect man.

Since it is a romantic comedy, one might forgive the moviemakers for exaggerating the actors' difference in stature and for glossing over some of the more serious aspects of height discrimination. It is refreshing that a short man was represented in a movie in a way that did not intentionally make the viewer feel sorry for him. It was also nice to see that although Ivana, her mother, and her ex-husband are depicted as struggling to accept him, throughout the movie other characters, such as his son and his ex-wife, show tremendous respect and understanding toward Leon and his condition. The success of *Corazon de Leon* inspired an almost identical movie remake from France called *Un Homme a la Hauteur (Up for Love)*, released in 2016.

Besides television shows and movies, commercials also frequently poke fun at short people by making unfavorable comparisons with taller people. One example is a Volkswagen commercial in which a tall woman is shown repeatedly encountering short men in various dating scenarios, with their height being a visible disappointment to her despite their physical attractiveness. These short men are depicted as unable to afford a car or taxi, since they must take her to these dates on foot, even in the pouring rain. The poor woman is forced to buy flats instead of the high-heeled shoes she really wants. At the end of the ad, another date arrives, driving up to pick her up in a vw car, and she thinks that because the car is small, it will be another second-rate short man. Instead, to her great relief, a taller man exits from the car. The woman appears to be very pleased to finally meet a date taller than herself. Apparently all the very attractive but short men she dated previously are not worthy of this woman, or of owning a vw.

Another commercial, made by Dairy Queen, begins with showing a young man sitting at one of the DQ restaurants and talking to the camera about the big chicken strip basket. He is apparently directing his remarks to a "big" construction worker, repeatedly pointing out what a big man he is. To demonstrate just how big he is, the construction worker says he is big enough to pick up his shorter coworker, who is standing next to him at the construction site. The "big" construction worker proceeds to pick him up despite being told that it is not necessary. The next scene shows the "big" construction worker literally having picked up the shorter man off the ground and holding him in his arms like a child. Then, in the following scene, the "big" worker is shown holding his shorter coworker as a man would hold a woman (in the same stance that Richard Gere used to carry Deborah Winger in the movie *An Officer and a Gentleman*). In only thirty seconds, this commercial managed to insult short men by comparing them not only to children, but also to women.

One long-running DirectTV ad was another blatant example of treating short men as inferior, childlike losers. In the ad, DirectTV presented a character called "Petite Randy Moss" as an alternative to the NFL wide receiver Randy Moss to represent how cable is inferior to DirectTV. This commercial depicted Petite Randy Moss in several humiliating situations, such as jumping up and down repeatedly to attempt to reach something on a high shelf at a store. Throughout the commercial the short Randy Moss is wearing some wrinkled shorts and a strange-looking sweater to make him look childlike and unkempt, while the tall Randy Moss is wearing a tailored business suit to enhance his perception as high-end, professional, and successful. The short Randy Moss seems confused and dumb, while the tall Randy Moss is calm and cool. The clear message is that short people are inferior and ridiculous, that there is something wrong with being short. Although most people found the ad hilarious, the message it was sending to short people is that they are losers. Had DirectTV used a racial minority or an overweight person to depict the less desirable cable, or someone with any other physical characteristic that is considered inferior, there would have been public indignation. Had the ad depicted any other marginalized group, there would have been serious repercussions. But because this ad involved making fun of height, nothing happened.

Certainly many physical features are depicted in a derogatory way in the media from time to time. However, when there is a derogatory depiction of any physical feature, however humorously done, it is usually considered offensive by most, unless it's about height. In fact, I struggled to find any other inherent physical trait that is treated with the same contempt or disrespect in the media as height, without a corresponding backlash. Sexist and racist depictions have been subjected to public indignation and anger, as have those that negatively depict overweight and LGBT individuals. But there has not been a comparable reaction to negative depictions of short people in the media. The message received by short people is that since there is no backlash of any kind against heightist representations, the audience must consider them a form of entertainment.

Even when a commercial has attempted to be complimentary to a short person, it nevertheless makes the point that being short is considered to be inferior by our society. In Tide's "Small Powerful" ads with gymnastics phenom Simone Biles, the commercial states: "*Although just four foot eight, Simone Biles is not to be underestimated. Despite her size,* Simone is packed with power." Another similar Tide commercial in the same series ends with these words: "*Surprisingly,* the most powerful gymnast is also the smallest."

Instead of focusing on Simone's strength and athleticism and her incredible performance as one of the most, if not the most, accomplished gymnasts in the world, Tide repeatedly focuses on her size, as though confirming that we all think being short equates to weakness and inadequacy. Otherwise, why should we be so surprised that short is powerful? Obviously Tide is attempting to compare Simone's smallness with strength in order to sell its detergent pods, but its message resonates with us because it really reflects our disbelief that someone that small could be so accomplished. This surprise is grounded in our prejudice that no one this small should be good at anything.

Even serious news programs are not immune to perpetuating height stereotypes. News coverage of gymnastics team's performance at the Rio Olympics repeatedly highlighted Simone's size as "diminutive," "tiny," "just four foot eight," the "smallest" on her team, and so forth, consistently pointing out her height to emphasize that her amazing performance is so amazing *despite* her size. In fact, Simone's small stature is actually an advantage in gymnastics. But the presumption is that the shorter someone is, the weaker and less competent he or she is expected to be. Hence our collective surprise when a short person displays strength and competence.

While it may be understandable that news programs would hone in on an athlete's size because her physique is related to her physical performance, the news coverage of the Rio Olympics did not continually harp on the height statistics of any athlete other than Simone. The only other athlete whose body proportions were a matter of any interest in Olympic coverage was Michael Phelps, much of which was to admire the length of his body in a complimentary way. Generally, the commentary about his body was focused on his proportions, his unusually long wingspan and a torso disproportionate to his height, described as the advantages that made him "built to be a swimmer." This commentary is in stark contrast to the commentary on Simone Biles's short stature, which mostly focused on the fact of her being *only* four foot eight. Rather than pointing out that Simone's compact body is "built to be a gymnast," or how her compact physicality affects her athleticism, the comments were focused on her height as a fact in and of itself, to make the point about how amazing it is that someone so small can be so good at gymnastics.

Serious news outlets have not limited their heightism to actors and athletes. Whenever a news story involves a short person, his or her height statistics become a worthy point of discussion in a way that they never would in a similar story about a person of average or tall height. And while other physical features like hair color, skin color, and nose size are typically not considered worthy of mention, when a short person is the subject of any type of news story, his or her height is declared as though it is somehow relevant. Usually, when the story is about an accomplished short person, his or her height is referenced to demonstrate how surprising it is that such an accomplished individual could be so small, typically with phrases such as "despite being only __ tall." If a similar story about a successful racial minority began with "despite being black," or a story about an accomplished obese person began with "despite weighing over __ pounds," it would provoke outrage, but when it comes to short people, citing their height is accepted as worthy of mention, even when the subject's height has absolutely no relevance to the story.

For instance, when Mother Teresa was declared a saint, news coverage repeatedly referenced her size, as though surprised that a person so small, under five feet tall, could be a Nobel prize winner or have left such a large legacy as a world-renowned humanitarian. The word *despite* was used frequently to reference her tiny size and her worldwide acclaim, in an effort to point out that this woman is extraordinary because her level of achievement is something that is typically outside the realm of possibility for a short-statured person. Why was it considered necessary to the story to mention her height at all? No other stories about other candidates for sainthood ever made a point to cite their size or describe their physical stature. Her faith, her service to the world's poor, and her status as a saint have absolutely nothing to do with her position on a height chart.

Similarly, news coverage about Supreme Court justice Ruth Bader Ginsburg frequently mentions the fact that she's "tiny" and "barely five feet tall." Even in articles praising her as a tough but fair champion for women's rights, her long list of accomplishments is often presented as a contrast to her physical stature. Similarly, coverage about her five-foot-three colleague Elena Kagan often reiterates how her mentor, Thurgood Marshall, nicknamed her "shorty." And the four-foot-eleven senator Barbara Boxer is frequently reported as carrying carts around to stand on while making speeches, because she is so "itty bitty." No other physical trait is reported on by the media as a fact that is worthy of being reported. When reporting on public figures, media never describe people by the shade of their skin, their hair and eye color, or their weight. Reports about average or taller public figures never cite their height statistics, because height is (and should be) completely irrelevant. The idea that serious news coverage even mentions height as a data point about accomplished and successful individuals confirms our perception that there is something incompatible about short people being accomplished and successful. We seem to be both amazed and amused by short people's accomplishments, as though physical stature had anything to do with them.

Not surprisingly, heightism is just as, if not more, pervasive in politics than in the social sphere. On July 7, 2014, the BBC news program described a joke in which David Cameron referred to John Bercow, the five-foot-six Speaker of the House of Commons, as one of the seven dwarves.[18] When John Bercow asked why making fun of someone's height should be considered appropriate, when mocking people based on race or sexual orientation is not, he was accused of making himself a victim in order to get publicity. The show concluded that height prejudice is morally acceptable because height discrimination is not protected by law.

The topic of height appears to be becoming more and more an object of fascination in politics, fueled largely by the media. Their obsession with height hit an all-time high during the 2016 presidential election in the United States. During the primaries much ado was made about the relative heights of the candidates, and numerous images were created representing all the candidates lined up against a height chart to emphasize their relative size. Because the public often goes along wherever the media lead, on the day of the first Republican debate, the candidates' heights were among the most-searched questions on the Internet. Several news outlets reported that the taller the candidate, the better his or her chances for success in the presidential election, referencing the oft-quoted report about the taller candidate winning almost 70 percent of presidential elections since the television era began.[19] Of course, as proven by the many short presidents who were elected before television existed, height is not related to intelligence, leadership, experience, or any other ability relevant to being president. The fact that our electorate is swayed by its height bias when it comes to selecting the leader of the country merely demonstrates the ignorance of the voters.

Unsurprisingly, Donald Trump took advantage of the public's basest instincts by mocking one of his rivals, Marco Rubio, calling him "little Marco" during a debate and otherwise putting down his size (despite the fact that Rubio is reported to be of average height at five foot ten). Although Trump has attacked everyone for everything, there was zero backlash against this; in fact, Trump gained support after making these comments. In contrast, after his first debate against Hillary Clinton, in which she revealed his offensive comments about a beauty pageant contestant being fat, the story generated a great deal of criticism and was covered by all the major news networks and newspapers for a week. Reports of the incident generally took the position that Trump's comments about the woman were wrong and insensitive and constituted body shaming.

Of course his comments about the contestant's weight were reprehensible, but consider that a beauty pageant contestant's weight is probably something that she was contractually obligated to maintain as a condition of participating in the pageant. Also, weight is something that is usually within a person's control, whereas height is not. Yet Trump's heightist remarks about Rubio did not lead to any criticism in the media. Instead of treating Trump's comments about Rubio's height at least as critically as his comments about the contestant's weight, media reporting actually contributed more fuel to Rubio's body shaming. Ann Coulter of Fox News was quoted as saying, "Rubio and Paul are as tall as my iPod" and are both too short to be president. Jeb Bush also took a shot at Rubio's size, telling MSNBC "at least I don't have a height issue." Much media attention was focused on the height of Rubio's boots, with one columnist saying, "Nice try, but you must be *this* tall to ride." The same reporter admired our shortest president, James Madison, pointing out that he was "itty bitty adorable five foot four" and declared that Americans are not prepared to elect a man who will be "followed by whispers of '*Oh, he's so much shorter than I thought.*'"[20]

Of course the results of both parties' primary elections bore out the theory that taller candidates usually win, resulting in the selection of an exceptionally tall candidate on each side. Donald Trump, at six foot two, is in the ninety-fifth percentile of heights for males his age (he and Jeb Bush tied as the two tallest candidates in the Republican primary). Hillary Clinton's height is reported as being anywhere between five foot five and five foot seven. If she is five foot seven as reported by most sources, Clinton is in the ninety-seventh percentile for women her age. Clinton's height itself has been a topic considered not too trivial to fascinate the media. A September 24, 2015, article by Jay Mathews in the esteemed *Washington Post* challenged her reported height of five foot seven, making the case that she is really closer to five foot five. Mathews even admitted to being "peculiar" enough to have chronicled the issue of height and its effects on U.S. politics, having written eight articles on the topic. Given that most of the reports claiming her height to be five foot seven cite each other as a source (but never question why her height is even a topic newsworthy enough to be a subject of coverage by serious news outlets), Mathews concluded that when compared visually to other candidates, she does not appear to be five foot seven, apparently ignoring the fact that a difference of two inches is visually very difficult to assess (and is probably affected by her wearing heels). But even at five foot five, Clinton would be in the seventy-fifth percentile for women her age, which is still very tall.

Of course the 2016 presidential election was most unusual in the types of topics that garnered media attention, particularly those surrounding Donald Trump. But despite the sheer number of *actually* serious issues that could have been covered, the media devoted an inordinate amount of coverage to the issue of the relative heights of the candidates. There were even articles about Hillary Clinton's efforts to mitigate the height difference between her and Donald Trump by using a custom lectern so that she could appear to be the same height as Trump. Sadly, many serious news reporters have failed to meet their obligation to educate and inform the public and continue to focus more and more on topics like height, which should be totally irrelevant to the issue of whether a person is qualified to be president of the United States.

Perhaps the worst representations of the social and cultural attitudes toward short people can be found in social media. Social networking services such as Twitter, Tumblr, and Reddit are replete with outrageous comments, most often directed at short men, but sometimes at women, too. Some observations are downright vicious and hateful, reflecting utter contempt and disregard, including declarations that short men should die or kill themselves or similar sentiments. Words like *midget* and *manlet* are commonly used to overtly mock and degrade others. Rather than receiving a backlash, as one would expect in a forum that invites an exchange of ideas, it is those who speak out against this treatment who are subjected to backlash and scolding.

These are just a few examples of the narrative that short people endure in our culture, the story that lends support to bullies in our schools and in the workplace, causing hardship in making friends and finding jobs and leading to isolation and depression for too many.

## NO SMALL INJUSTICE

Coupled with the incessant media message that being short is inferior, our natural bias, which leads us to associate tallness with power and superiority, has led to some serious consequences in how people interact with each other and how short people perceive themselves. Short people routinely experience difficulties in being hired and promoted and often earn significantly less money than tall people for doing the same jobs. Some parents have put their young and healthy but short children through years of hormone treatment in an effort to make them taller, hoping that their children will avoid facing the social stigma associated with short stature. Many short teens and adults experience low self-esteem and depression, which can sometimes be so severe that the person withdraws from friends, family, and normal life pursuits.

The depression associated with social heightism has led some to commit suicide. In May 2015 British reality TV star Jonathan McNally hanged himself at age twenty-seven after having struggled with depression about his height.[21] His family said he had been depressed since age fifteen due to being small, even though he had eventually grown to five foot seven. News stories about teenage boys committing suicide due to bullying for being small have not been uncommon, including an Irish boy named Joseph Morris, age thirteen, whose suicide note explained that he did it because he was tired of being teased about his height.[22] Another thirteen-year-old, Jonathon Short-Scaff from Ohio, committed suicide in July 2014 after years of being bullied for being small.[23] The day before, bullies at school had told him to go kill himself. Previous complaints by his mother to his school's principal about bullying had had no effect. In May 2013 twelve-year-old Joel Morales of New York hanged himself after two years of unrelenting physical and emotional torment about being small and brainy.[24] Despite multiple complaints to school officials, the teasing had continued unabated. In September 2014 Lamar Hawkins, a fourteen-year-old from Florida, committed suicide in his school bathroom after being relentlessly bullied by his classmates because of his small size.[25] Unfortunately these boys are not the only ones, or even the youngest, to have killed themselves. On September 19, 2016, Jackson Grubb from West Virginia, only nine years old, hanged himself after having endured months of bullying for being little.[26]

To alleviate their plight and the severe social stigma, some short people have gone to extremes, resorting to limb-lengthening surgery, in which a surgeon divides the leg bones into sections and the patient suffers excruciating pain while the bones gradually grow back together into a complete but longer bone. This procedure is expensive—anywhere from $25,000 to $175,000—gruesome, and agonizingly painful. It can take up to two years for patients to recover from it. There are several forums on the Internet that discuss this procedure, including many photographs and journals of patients. Comments typically include descriptions of the social stigma, humiliation, and workplace hardships that have steered some people to pursue such a painful solution. Infections and other serious complications are very common, especially when this procedure is performed on patients of short stature, rather than patients who have a limb length discrepancy.[27] Some people, seeking to save money, have traveled abroad to countries such as China, India, and Russia to have this procedure, sometimes returning crippled or requiring even more surgeries to correct poor results. This limb-lengthening procedure is more analogous to a medieval torture technique than a proper medical procedure and should be the stuff of science fiction horror movies, not a serious medical consideration for people who are short but otherwise healthy.

One article describes Komal, a twenty-four-year old Indian woman who was four foot six prior to the surgery.[28] She had to sell her family's ancestral lands to pay for the expensive surgery, but she felt that it was worth it to avoid ridicule and get a better job. In India the surgery is un-regulated, and many surgeons have no proper training in the procedure. Dr. Sudhir Kapoor, the president of the Indian Orthopaedic Association, was reported as saying that while the surgery should be performed only in very rare cases, and he himself had wondered whether it was the right thing to do, he had decided it was worth it because of the transformation in his patients' self-esteem.[29]

Such extreme and misguided attempts to correct a social bias by medically treating the victim would not be necessary if there were more awareness of the social bias and if short people were treated with dignity and respect. The children who bullied those boys who ended up committing suicide, the people who bully those who feel compelled to subject themselves to excruciating pain just to be a little bit taller, all live in societies in which degrading people for their short stature is acceptable. We are bombarded daily with millions of messages in our schools, at work, on television, in the movies, in the news, and on the Internet that short individuals are comical and inferior, that short people just don't matter. And it should not be surprising that many of us who are recipients of these reminders cannot help but internalize this message. It is inevitable that many short people will come to believe that they will never be taken seriously and that there is no reason to feel hope. A response like that is completely logical.

Certainly most short people consider the hardships they face inconvenient but manageable. Being short does not mean automatically being doomed to a miserable life. People can and do make adjustments and overcome obstacles so they can go on with the more important aspects of their lives. Many short people have achieved great success and recognition. Many lead productive lives and are just as happy and well-adjusted as taller people. But the road to becoming well-adjusted can be a bumpy and unpleasant one, and for some it never happens. One may say that overcoming hardship builds character; tell that to those whose severe depression led them to commit suicide, such as Jonathan McNally, Joseph Morris, Jonathon Short-Scaff, Joel Morales, Lamar Hawkins, and Jackson Grubb. If child suicide is insufficient for heightism to be taken seriously, what will it take?

The more important question is why short people should be forced to adapt to such senseless prejudice and even to unnecessary everyday inconveniences. Just because certain short people have managed to achieve great success does not mean that we should not demand full acceptance and dignity for all short people.

Heightism may not seem as bad as some other ills in this world. Certainly many people in the world endure far worse suffering, and most people are not strangers to some form of prejudice. But a small injustice should not be overshadowed by a bigger one. In fact there is no valid reason to compare different forms of prejudice against each other. Yes, heightism is similar to racism and sexism in that it is also based on an inherent physical trait that cannot be changed or concealed. Like women and racial minorities, short people are regarded by many in our culture as subordinate and inferior. One may argue that heightism is at least as prevalent as or more prevalent than discrimination based on ethnicity, weight, or sexual orientation, because those aspects are capable of being concealed or changed.

But all of that is really irrelevant. Different forms of discrimination can exist alongside each other, and some forms of prejudice can be more severe, but that does not make other prejudices irrelevant. Comparing different forms of prejudice and trying to decide which is worse than another is an exercise in futility, and it misses the point. Some prejudices are more severe; some are more prevalent. The point is, prejudice is prejudice, and it does not matter how similar or different biases are. Heightism may not be as severe as racism or sexism, but it can feel just as hurtful to its victims. Our human dignity deserves that all bigotry be addressed.

One difference between heightism and other forms of discrimination is that the other forms of discrimination are openly acknowledged by everyone, while in our culture heightism is widespread and unhindered. There are virtually no laws protecting short people against employment discrimination based on height. There are hardly any advocates to stand up and speak out against the humiliation and degradation that routinely occur in schools, in movies, on television shows, and in social media. Moreover, heightism is not even recognized as a real social issue, even by those who are otherwise champions of social justice. No one even wants to talk about heightism as a fact of life. We generally do not admit that it even exists. When confronted with it, we are surprised that someone might accuse us of doing anything wrong. We tend to treat it as a trivial nonissue. On the rare occasion that the subject of height discrimination is brought up in conversation, people usually assume it is a joke. The topic tends to generate either eye rolling or patronizing amusement. Most would consider the idea of height discrimination a ridiculous notion not worthy of serious discussion. This indifference to short people's experience is devastating.

But just as white people may not recognize certain incidents as examples of racism, and just as men may not recognize certain incidents as offensive toward women, tall and average height individuals may not recognize heightism when they see it. That does not mean that heightism does not exist or is not a real issue. The fact that most people are ignorant about it does not make it trivial or irrelevant. Heightism is no less important than sexism, racism, or homophobia and deserves no less discussion and study. We long ago realized the injustice toward women and racial minorities and resolved to address them. Racism and sexism have come to be viewed as social afflictions that demand redress. Fighting for equal rights under the law as well as dignity and respect in the social sphere has become widely accepted and deemed a respectable pursuit. However, heightism is largely unknown or ignored as a cause. While there are thousands of books, articles, movies, television shows, and college courses discussing aspects of various "-isms," there has been very little discussion about prejudice based on height. Only a handful of books and a smattering of articles discuss the topic, and there is not a single college course on it. Despite the fact that there are millions of people in the United States who are considered extremely short, there is virtually no debate regarding whether their experience in our culture merits study and correction. There are not nearly the number of Web sites or support organizations devoted to addressing prejudice toward short people as there are to addressing other real or perceived social ills. Only a couple of support Web sites exist on the Internet, and they mostly focus on support for short males related to dating concerns.

The time has come to bring attention to and raise awareness of an issue that has been long overlooked. The fact that little has been written about height discrimination does not mean that it does not deserve to be the subject of public discourse, just like racism, sexism, and other -isms. The fact that height discrimination is not currently prohibited by federal law does not mean it does not exist or does not matter. There was a time in our country's recent past when race and sex discrimination were not prohibited by law, when most men (and many women) believed that a woman's only rightful place was in the home and that black people should not be allowed to drink from the same water fountains or sit at the same service counters as white people. But our society no longer accepts these views as right or moral. While such beliefs may still be held by some, they are considered extremist and inappropriate by most people. Just because it used to be legal to discriminate against people on the basis of sex or race does not mean that it is moral or right to do so, as is widely recognized and accepted today.

Heightism is a social ill that negatively affects millions of people who deserve to be treated with dignity and respect. We have a duty to attempt to rid the world of this senseless prejudice. The time has come for a change in how short people are treated in our society. All short people, both those who have overcome bigotry and those who are still struggling with it, deserve to live in a society that rejects it.

Words like *discrimination* and *prejudice* can make some people uncomfortable and often cause negative reactions. When these words are used, people begin to focus on what they mean for them. It is easier to become defensive, argue, or ignore something than it is to learn how other people are impacted. If we cannot talk productively about it, we will not be able to fix the problem. It is lack of awareness that has allowed these issues to persist, so we need to accept that these words will be used as a means to learn from past mistakes and bring about lasting change.

# height discrimination against children

WITHOUT REALIZING IT consciously, we seem to be preoccupied with our children's physical size. Parents are endlessly and inexplicably fascinated by comparing their children's height and growth to those of other children. One of the first things that new parents announce about their newborn babies are the length and weight statistics. At well-baby visits to the pediatrician, parents eagerly await the doctor's plotting of their child's latest growth data on the growth chart. Parents often continue their own statistical gathering and monitoring of a child's height measurements on a door frame in their homes, collecting and documenting this aspect of their child's growth and development more frequently than all others—usually well into the child's adolescence.

When meeting with other parents at school or on the playground, parents compare their children's height and weight percentiles. The parents whose children fall in the upper percentiles for height display significantly more pride about their kids' size than those parents whose children are in the lower percentiles. It is as though a child's tallness is some sort of achievement worth celebrating. Parents who spend that much time bragging about their children's academic, athletic, or creative endeavors are viewed as show-offs, but no one questions parents who boast about their children's tallness.

The social stigma attached to short stature is unique in this way, because parents openly and bluntly express delight when their children are tall in a way that they would never do regarding other inherent traits that have been compared and deemed inferior. Parents generally do not openly announce their babies' racial statistics in birth announcements or bluntly compare their babies with others based on the relative lightness or darkness of their skin color. They usually do not consider their child's blond hair or blue eyes as a cause to feel pride in the same way that they do when the child is tall. What ought to be considered a trivial physical feature has acquired a significance that is much more profound than a mere genetic trait. How did this preoccupation with height develop, and why does it persist?

## HOW TALL IS YOUR FETUS?

The measuring tape comes out of the drawer even before a baby is born. As early as the twentieth week of pregnancy and at each subsequent prenatal visit, doctors begin measuring the fundal height of the pregnant woman's belly and recording the dimensions in the medical chart. This method involves measurement of the maternal abdomen from the pubic bone to the uterine fundus with a tape measure. The purpose is to assess the size and growth of the fetus, to see if it is compatible with the "normal" range for that gestational age.

Detecting potential abnormalities in fetal growth and other complications is the whole point of prenatal care. However, this particular technique is neither useful nor reliable;[1] first, no one really knows how the "normal" range was determined; second, studies have shown that the vast majority (80 percent) of babies who were born either small or large for their gestational age were not identified as such by prebirth fundal measurements; and third, the measurements themselves have anywhere from 17 to 93 percent accuracy, with an average of 65 percent. Such a lack of precision indicates that fundal measurement has little, if any, scientific or medical value. Furthermore, an abnormal finding is usually nothing to worry about. A too-large belly is likely to be caused by fluid retention or simply being a bigger woman before pregnancy. A belly that is too small usually signifies nothing serious, the most likely scenario being that the fetus is small, in which case nothing can really be done about it.

Along with ultrasounds and sonograms, the mother's nutritional condition throughout pregnancy is a far more important and accurate gauge for assessing the development and health of the fetus. There is a widely accepted premise that a strong link exists between birth weight and later health. There is no link whatsoever associated with a baby's length and later health. Given that, one might question the scientific value of even taking a tape measurement of fundal height. As long as the mother is careful about her nutritious intake and receives excellent prenatal care, and the baby is developing according to gestational age based on ultrasound and sonogram analysis, what does it matter how "tall" the belly is?

Unfortunately, performing this measurement takes considerable time during each prenatal visit and causes unnecessary worry and concern for the expectant mother. What little value the practice of measuring the fundal height may add to the medical assessment is far outweighed by the negative social stereotyping created and perpetuated about the unborn child's relative size and length. The one thing this practice does accomplish quite effectively is to begin to form an impression in the expectant mother's mind of the doctor's perception of the high impor-tance of the baby's size. Even though when asked doctors will deny the importance or accuracy of the measurement, the message received by the expectant mother is that the doctor considers these data to be very important. As sensitive as pregnant women are to every little aspect of their pregnancies, they cling to and focus on their doctor's every action, word, body language, and facial expression. They interpret the doctor's activities at the medical visit as obviously important, or else the doctor would not bother doing them. As a result, expectant mothers adopt the attitude that the size of their fetus must be something very significant, something that they need to be concerned about. If the cues are positive, expectant mothers revel in their child's favorable placement; if the cues are even a little bit tentative, or if they happen to fall outside the "normal" range (for which there is no scientific basis), they begin to worry about these measurements.

So begins the size obsession that lasts throughout our lives. Almost as soon as the baby is delivered, its length and weight are recorded. As long as there is no real medical emergency involving the baby's health, measuring the baby is the first thing that occurs after delivery, sometimes even before the baby is placed in the mother's arms for the first time. This measuring is done with great urgency, as if the failure to record the actual length and weight within the first few seconds of life might lead to having missed out on something essential. What if the baby has a growth spurt within the first hour of life, before those first measurements are recorded? Then all our future data collection will be for naught. We will never really know what was the true base measurement and will skew all of our subsequent efforts to assess growth.

The preoccupation about size during the first moments of life is not the end of this obsession. The initial measuring of a baby at birth launches a routine that lasts throughout childhood. After birth, at the beginning of every visit to the pediatrician's office, the weight and height are measured and plotted on an official-looking chart. It is often the first item of business before anything else is done, before the child's temperature is taken, before the child's health is assessed in any other way. The child's percentile is declared and becomes one of the primary descriptors of the child's position within (or outside) the norm.

If only those statistics were treated as a charming tradition, they would be harmless enough. But the tradition is both a cause and a symptom of our unconscious concern about our children's relative size and percentile compared to other children. This concern, in turn, has an impact on our perceptions about size within our cultural norm that lasts well into adulthood. If a baby's statistics are not perceived as "normal" based on socially acceptable ranges, then parents do not proclaim them in birth announcements. Parents of short kids often experience shame, anxiety, and disappointment. Parents whose children fall on the extreme edges of the growth charts experience many negative emotions, among which is a concern about the societal prejudices their children will suffer related to size and height. Parents expend a great deal of energy worrying and hoping that their children will be tall enough, but do not seem to consider: tall enough for what? The answer is: tall enough to be treated with respect, to be considered not invisible. We do not wish to acknowledge that the reason for all the worrying is rooted in societal discrimination, and that the only way to combat the problem is to fight the discrimination rather than merely hope for our children to be tall.

It is amazing that the human race managed to survive for millennia before the practice of recording our children's height was adopted and became commonplace. And we persist in this obsession with gathering this particular statistic over and above data points related to other physical traits. Even throughout adulthood, doctors continue to record their patients' height in the medical record at every doctor's visit, despite the fact that our height does not change much after we reach adulthood, and there is rarely any medical usefulness for this information.

## CHARTING GROWTH

The current reference pediatric growth charts, which are used by most pediatric offices, were developed by the Centers for Disease Control (CDC). They show a representation of the height of children of the same age and gender in the United States. They include clear demarcation lines showing the "normal" range, which is represented between the fifth and ninety-fifth percentiles (some charts reflect the range between the third and ninety-seventh percentiles). The range depicted in these charts is the "statistical normal" distribution based on the standard deviation bell curve of the population of children in the United States; it is not based on a medical assessment of what is considered "normal."

Most parents eagerly anticipate the pediatrician's arrival in the exam room so that they can see where he or she will plot their child's growth on the chart. They want to see whether their child falls into the "normal" range and which percentile band their child occupies on the curve. What most parents fail to realize is that the standard growth charts do not accurately reflect the true range of normality with respect to natural differences in velocity of growth and rates of maturation. The charts say absolutely nothing about growth *rates;* they merely represent a survey of heights in a population at a certain point in time.[2]

Growth charts cannot accurately reflect the growth of all children because there is an enormous range of what is normal and healthy in the natural variation of the human species. Children come in a variety of shapes and sizes, and their growth rates vary widely. This variability is not just among individual children, but also can be found among different nationalities and ethnicities, as well as over periods of time. One boy may be smaller than his peers because he is maturing at a slower rate but will eventually grow to be an average-height man. Another boy may be the same size as the first but is maturing at an average rate and will always be of small stature. One girl may be very tall because both her parents are of Nordic heritage, while another girl of the same age may be very short because her parents are both Hispanic. All of these children are otherwise perfectly healthy. None of them is abnormal. Yet many parents of such children would experience great stress and anxiety, and unfortunately, many doctors would respond with unnecessary medical testing and intervention. Unfortunately, the huge variability in growth rates among children of different races and ethnic groups makes it impossible to create a perfect growth chart that accurately represents the true range of what is "normal" growth, leading to an overreliance on the standard growth charts and a great deal of unwarranted concern about an individual child's growth.

Growth charts were not designed to be used as tools for evaluating individuals, but rather to show general patterns of heights in a given population. A growth chart is a very simplistic, imprecise tool that does not deserve the trust we have placed in it. It should be considered nothing more than a tool that shows a child's current height and weight, as well as how fast he or she is growing over time: a rudimentary indication of the child's health. It may be an acceptable means to satisfy curiosity for those who do fall within the normal range, but for those who do not, it is more than worthless—it can be quite damaging. Our obsession with height measuring has come to mean something much more significant than what some might assume is harmlessly using a crude tool to measure a child's overall health. For those children on the lower end of the growth chart, or those whose height is below the lowest curve on the chart, it has come to represent a lower social or cultural status, accompanied by a substantial psychological impact.

Growth charts are less helpful than they are anxiety producing. They provide little value for those children who are developing within the cultural norm, but they encourage parents to worry and cause guilt on the part of the parents who have short children. The charts often fuel competitiveness by inciting parents to compare their children to others. The doctors' focus on measuring height does little to aid in identifying serious medical issues, but it superficially elevates the importance of stature in the minds of parents and fosters our societal biases, to the detriment of children who happen to be outside of this arbitrary "normal" range. It is no wonder, then, that parents become so focused on and concerned about their children's placement on the growth chart. While scientists may have had good intentions in using this apparently objective way to measure children, they have unwittingly created and continue to perpetuate a social bias against the individuals whose measurements are plotted on the remote ends of the charts. It has produced a "lasting fear of deviation, in both children and parents, about a temporary biological situation, [making] height more of an issue than it might otherwise be."[3]

In addition to imprecise reference data depicted on the growth charts used by most pediatricians, the height measurements themselves are often very inaccurate. One study found that more than 70 percent of height measurements done in family practice centers in the United

States are inaccurate.[4] Many doctors' offices do not use a stadiometer or other accurate measuring equipment to determine height, or they use improper measuring techniques, such as measuring children with shoes on.[5] Sometimes even measurements done carefully two or three times in a row are inaccurate; the numbers should be the same, but they are not. Such lack of accuracy in measurements could not only negatively affect a child psychologically, it also could lead to potential problems in determining whether growth is abnormal. It could lead doctors to miss a growth problem or to unnecessarily worry parents and order medical treatment for a problem that does not exist. Together with the simplistic CDC growth charts, the unscientific measuring techniques used by most pediatric offices have contributed to unnecessary parental anxiety about children who are, by every truly scientific and medical assessment, perfectly healthy and normal.

The fact that the child's height and weight are the first things that are measured and plotted during a doctor's visit and that this procedure takes up a disproportionate amount of the brief time parents have with the child's doctor puts the focus on the child's height and position on the growth chart as the most essential feature of the visit. It leads the parents to believe that the assessment and monitoring of the child's height is supremely significant. Would parents be so preoccupied with their children's stature if the pediatricians' offices put a little less emphasis on it? Is it truly *the* most important factor about a child's development, surpassing all other health issues?

Our overemphasis on measuring, plotting, and comparing children's size has consequences for how we view growth and height. It has a significant impact on parents' perception of their child's stature and affects their behavior toward the child. Parents of a short child often begin worrying about all the societal problems the child will encounter as a result of being short. Whether intentionally or subconsciously, this worrying is conveyed to the child. Parents begin to act differently and treat the child differently. Adults are constantly drumming the importance of height into children with comments about how much they have grown and how they need to eat well so they can "grow up to be big and strong." A child learns to associate tallness with positive reinforcement and shortness with inadequacy. When a child seems to be failing to measure up, parents become anxious and panicky. They even pursue medical intervention, including growth hormones and sometimes even surgery—anything to avoid their child being fated to remain short.

Should all children have their growth and development monitored on a regular basis? Of course. If the child appears to be much shorter or much taller than most children his or her age, or if growth has decreased or stopped, there should be a medical evaluation to determine the cause. How the medical profession handles this process is what could be significantly improved. Doctors would do short children and our society a great service if they would place less emphasis on the measurements and growth charts and spend more time evaluating each child using common sense, such as whether he or she eats well and is developing appropriately. In addition, how measurements are taken and recorded, as well as the equipment that is used to take the measurements, must be improved. Pediatricians' offices must implement more accurate measuring techniques, including taking multiple measurements and using equipment that is capable of providing more precision than the standard equipment used in most offices.

The idea of using growth charts as a way to assess a child's growth and development is not a bad idea. However, if we are going to continue to rely on growth charts, doctors should take the time to place the charts in proper context for the parents, and we should insist on better growth charts that depict the true diversity of the human race. Rather than using the standard CDC growth charts currently available, doctors should begin using multiple sets of charts that show the real variety of potential growth based on different maturation trajectories (slow, average, late) and showing separate ranges for gender, race, locality, and ethnic group. Such charts were developed and used in Europe in the 1960s[6] and could be adopted and modified for use in the United States without a large investment of time or resources. Having better, more accurate charts would help demonstrate to parents that size differences during childhood and adolescence tend to resolve themselves naturally.

It would alleviate unnecessary parental concern and medical intervention. Avoiding unnecessary medical testing and treatments would save our overburdened health system millions of dollars each year.

## ABNORMALLY HEALTHY

Extremely short stature can be caused by a wide variety of factors, both medical and natural. There are some serious diseases and genetic conditions that accompany extremely short stature, such as Down and Turner syndromes, genetic syndromes, bone and skeletal disorders, hormonal disorders such as hypothyroidism and growth hormone deficiency, celiac disease, and certain kidney disorders.[7] These are critical medical conditions, but they are extremely rare. Severe undernutrition also can cause short stature. However, this book is not about patients who have such medical conditions, which are a serious matter that must be addressed with doctors. It is usually quite obvious to the naked eye that a child has a serious medical condition such as these, even without the aid of our compulsive focus on down-to-the-fraction-of-an-inch height measuring. Stature is merely one of the many indicators that doctors look for when evaluating whether a patient has one of these conditions, and it is certainly not the only or the most important factor.

Although most people suspect that a child's short stature must be due to an underlying disorder or pathology, in fact, severe short stature is not usually a sign of a health problem and often has no medical cause. It is exceedingly rare for short stature alone, absent any other symptoms, to indicate a serious health problem. Only 5 percent of children who are in the bottom 5 percent of the height curve have an actual medical condition that is the underlying cause of the short stature.[8] For such children, medical intervention is necessary. The vast majority of extremely short children—the other 95 percent of the fifth percentile—are short due to a growth delay, genetics, or a combination of the two.

Constitutional growth delay occurs when children are small for their age but are growing at a normal rate, and they will eventually reach an adult height within the normal range. They are simply slow to mature.

These children typically have a normal birth height, but within two years of birth their height dips to below the fifth percentile, and they tend to grow slowly, reach puberty later than their peers, and keep growing to a later age than their peers.[9]

Genetically short stature, also called familial short stature, is the second common cause of extreme short stature. A child in this category is short because one or both parents are short. These children typically are growing at a normal rate, parallel to but at or below the "normal" curve, and they usually end up being short adults, like their parents.[10] Constitutional growth delay and familial short stature (or a combination of the two) are the causes for 95 percent of extremely short stature.

Children who are short due to constitutional growth delay or genetics are perfectly healthy and normal. Given the nature of the statistic principle of the bell curve, there will *always* be individuals in any population who will fall within the bottom 5 percent, so it is wrong to call their height "abnormal." But unfortunately, abnormal is how they are perceived, and the medical profession has promoted this perception and allowed it to persist.

In the process of determining whether extremely short children might fall into the *unhealthy* 5 percent of the 5 percent, pediatricians usually refer them to pediatric endocrinologists. During several visits, the child endures numerous detailed measurements of the torso, hands, feet, and limbs; complete medical examinations of the body including the child's genitalia; exposure to X-rays; and comprehensive investigations of family history. In addition, the child usually must undergo stimulation testing lasting several hours to measure the amount of insulin-like growth hormone-I (IGF-I) in the blood. A series of blood tests is performed to measure concentrations of various hormones in the blood and the ability of the pituitary gland to respond to various stimuli. Because the pituitary gland produces growth hormone in bursts, the level of growth hormone in a single random blood sample is likely to be very low. To test for growth hormone deficiency, therefore, several blood samples are obtained over a period of time. Since a child may not respond to any given test on a given day, more than one stimulus may be needed to evaluate the child's ability to produce growth hormone, involving hospitalizing the child and measuring the amount of growth hormone present in blood samples obtained overnight during sleep or even during an entire twenty-four-hour period.

Once all these procedures, some of which are quite invasive, are completed, 95 percent of these children should be given a clean bill of health. Unfortunately, either parental pressure or the need to justify all the medical resources already expended leads doctors to want to make the process seem worthwhile. Rather than using the already-existing terms "constitutional growth delay" or "familial short stature," doctors have created a new diagnosis for these 95 percent of short children: idiopathic short stature. It is a diagnosis given to children whose testing fails to reveal a medical cause for their short stature.

The term *idiopathic* literally means "of unknown cause, as a disease." This label only serves to harm short but healthy children, because there is nothing medically wrong with them. Giving their stature a medical-sounding designation like *idiopathic* leads people to believe that it is some kind of condition or disease that requires medical attention. The suffix "-pathic" is of Greek origin, meaning one who suffers, a victim. The *Merriam-Webster Medical Dictionary* defines the word *disease* as "an impairment of the normal state of the body or one of its parts that interrupts or modifies the performance of the vital functions." When the term *idiopathic* is used to describe other medical conditions, it refers to actual medical disorders or incorrectly functioning systems of the body. Following are some examples:

> *Idiopathic aplastic anemia* is a condition in which the bone marrow fails to properly make blood cells.
> *Idiopathic pulmonary fibrosis* is a lung disease involving the progressive and fatal scarring of the lungs.
> *Essential hypertension* is also known as primary or idiopathic hypertension.

In contrast, being short but healthy is not a medical condition. It is not abnormal for 5 percent of the population to be on the bottom and top ends of the bell curve; it is this normal range of human heights that the statistical curve represents. Idiopathic short stature is not a disease at all; it is of no medical significance. Short children who have idiopathic short stature are no different intellectually, psychosocially, or academically from children whose height is within the normal range.[11] Children with idiopathic short stature have no apparent defects in hormone production, secretion, or action and have no dysfunction or disability. They are simply shorter than the median height of the general population. They are healthy and normal and might actually have been within a normal range of heights if they had been born in another culture where the standard distribution is centered around a shorter median value.

The height distribution chart is just an arbitrary representation of the most commonplace range of heights in our particular country. To be on the extreme edge of this chart does not automatically signify that one has any medical condition at all. Since the entire bell curve of heights is a standard distribution—otherwise known as normal distribution— there is no such thing as "abnormal" when it comes to heights unless there is a medical condition at the root. An outlier on the distribution chart is not abnormal; in contrast, it is perfectly normal to have a small percentage of values on the distribution be outliers. To label a short child with a medical diagnosis simply because of a statistical depiction of one country's height distribution is confounding and may even *border on the unethical.*

The diagnosis of idiopathic short stature and the frequent and obsessive measuring and plotting of the child's height on the standard growth charts do short children a tremendous disservice that carries long-lasting impacts throughout their lives. The fact that these children happen to deviate from the mean by too many inches means they are too different, to the point of being "abnormal." Parents often assume that short children have some kind of disability; they battle feelings of guilt, blaming themselves for producing short children who will be forced to suffer in life.

This in turn leads to a series of negative consequences. The experience of being taken to the doctor is itself often a bad memory, leaving feelings of having been humiliated, poked, and prodded. It sends the message to children that the people they trust most in their lives—their parents and their doctor—believe that they are abnormal, that there is something seriously wrong with them. Even if the doctor confirms that there is nothing wrong physically, both the parents and the children still come away feeling there is something wrong, because the label of *idiopathic* implies the presence of a disease or medical condition. It highlights that these children are shorter than (read: inferior to) most or all of the other children. These children inevitably will begin to internalize these judgments and begin to believe that medical intervention is necessary to address their abnormality.

The experience also causes parents to worry about the child's prospects in our prejudiced society and to try to do something to "fix" the nonexistent problem. They make even more appointments with pediatric endocrinologists to get second and third opinions, at which the child is measured in even greater detail, tested in ways that are intimidating and humiliating for a young child. Many parents will even request or insist on unnecessary growth hormone treatment for children who have no medical need for it.

## GROWTH HORMONE THERAPY

Most people would consider it a great idea to get their short children some human growth hormone (hGH) to attempt to help them grow taller, even when there is no evidence that their bodies are not producing adequate amounts of hGH on their own. After all, hGH occurs naturally in the body, so what harm could there be in adding a little extra? Human growth hormone promotes development of bone, muscle mass, and the cells that support the growth and repair of internal organs and tissues. Various levels of the hormone are produced by the body throughout a person's lifetime. Without sufficient hGH, a child will not be able to reach his or her full potential height.

Since 1958, children whose bodies do not produce adequate amounts of their own growth hormone have received treatment with hGH as a medical response to their medical condition. The hormone increases the heights of such hormone-deficient children, but typically, such children nevertheless remain much shorter than average. When this treatment first came into use, hGH was extracted from cadavers. The supply of hGH was so limited that only the neediest children were provided with the treatment. In 1985 it was discovered that some of the hGH had been contaminated, having been extracted from a cadaver infected with Creutzfeldt-Jakob disease, which causes rapid brain degeneration leading to death within a year of the first appearance of symptoms. The disease can lie dormant for decades after exposure, and there is no test or treatment for it. Eventually, twenty-six people died from contaminated hGH; as a consequence, the use of hGH sourced from cadavers was discontinued after the mid-1980s.

Coincidentally around the same time, hGH had begun to be manufactured using recombinant bacteria. Within six months of the ban on the cadaver-sourced hGH, bioengineered hGH began to be mass produced without resorting to cadavers. In order to get this product to the market, the pharmaceutical companies embarked on a campaign to acquire U.S. Food and Drug Administration (FDA) approval of hGH therapy for idiopathic short children. Before then, only about one in two hundred children below the third percentile was identified as having an actual growth hormone deficiency.[12] If hGH treatment was limited only to those with a true medical need for the hormone, then there would be insufficient financial incentive for these companies to pursue manufacturing it. To make a profit, it was convenient to make shortness a disease to create demand for the treatment.[13] By including children who were short but otherwise healthy, the potential target market increased considerably: even targeting only the bottom 1.2 percentile on the growth chart would equate to about 400,000 children. It was around that time that the term *idiopathic short stature* came into use; before then, short but normal children were simply described as having "short normal stature" or "familial short stature."

Beginning in 1988 and continuing until 2001, the National Institutes of Health (NIH) and the pharmaceutical company Eli Lily funded an experiment to see if hGH treatment would be both safe and effective for children with idiopathic short stature who did not have a growth hormone deficiency. Hundreds of healthy children were subjected to a study to determine whether hGH was safe. Participation in the study involved subjecting the children to multiple blood tests over various periods; urine tests; stool tests; X-rays; MRIs; photographs with clothes off; and various behavioral, dietary, and social service evaluations.[14] It required three days of testing in a hospital setting to determine if a child was qualified to participate in this study, and only children who were found to have no abnormalities or physical basis for their short stature were invited—in other words, only perfectly healthy children were included in the study. Once enrolled in the study, some children received injections of hGH while some received injections of a placebo. The study continued until the child's final adult height was attained, when the child was between fifteen and eighteen years old, an average participation of four to seven years.

If these children experienced any issues with confidence and self-image prior to their participation in this study, then the humiliation of submitting to nude photographs and urine and stool samples, coupled with the intimidation of multiple blood tests, spending time in hospitals and clinics instead of going to school, and years of daily injections, no doubt worsened any such negative self-image. The fact that the study began with seventy-one subjects and ended with only thirty-three illustrates how intrusive and off-putting participants found the experience. The large dropout rate raises questions about the reliability of the results reported by the researchers.

The results of the study showed that after an average of four years of treatment, the subjects' final adult height increased by an average of one and one-half inches from expected adult height, which was predicted at the initiation of participation in the study. The study failed to show that hGH treatment improved the subjects' psychosocial adjustment or quality of life in any way. Throughout the study, the NIH continued to refer to these children as abnormal or suffering from a disorder. In co-funding the study with a pharmaceutical company that stood to make considerable profits from sales of hGH to short but healthy children, the NIH promoted a path for FDA approval for an unnecessary treatment. It was grossly irresponsible to test healthy human subjects for the benefit of private corporations while not having full knowledge of the long-term health risks to the subjects. The NIH study contributed to the medicalization of a social problem, assuming that the adding of inches to a child's height would address the bias against short stature in our culture. It is unimaginable that the NIH would embark on a similar study designed to test skin lightening treatments for dark-skinned children or hormone treatment for brown-eyed children to make their eyes blue. But our societal assumptions and ignorance about height made it seem acceptable to study hormone treatments to make short children taller.

Prior to 2003, the FDA had approved the use of hGH for use only in hormone-deficient children and for other limited indications of actual medical disorders, such as renal insufficiency. However, the pharmaceutical companies discovered that healthy short children are a big and infinite market and encouraged doctors to prescribe it for off-label uses. To put things in perspective, in the United States an estimated 1,062,000 children have idiopathic short stature, but only 24,000 have medically defined short stature.[15] The pharmaceutical companies found the need to go after a greater and unlimited demand for their product. The profit motive was powerful and irresistible: with treatment lasting between five and ten years at $20,000–$40,000 per year, they were hoping for annual profits to exceed $2 billion per year.

Expanding the population to children with idiopathic short stature was necessary to ensure a large enough and constantly self-replenishing market for their product. Even if the entire current population of children in the fifth percentile is "cured" of short stature, the mean height of the distribution curve will shift to the right, thereby creating a new group of patients that will fall into the fifth percentile. In other words, using hGH to increase the heights of very short children creates the need to reclassify previously normal children as severely short and thus in need of hGH treatment—so treatment of one group creates illness in another previously healthy group, repeatedly creating a new set of patients.

With encouragement from pharmaceutical companies, in July 2003 the FDA approved the use of hGH for treatment of children with idiopathic short stature despite the extremely modest effectiveness of treatment—increasing height by one and one-half inches after four years of treatment, estimated to be more than what the person would have obtained without treatment. (As we explore later, such estimates are not based on very scientific measurement or predictions, and there is no way to know with any certainty that the same growth would not have occurred naturally.)

The FDA approval of hGH treatment was pushed by the pharmaceutical companies based on the assumption that short people suffer from psychological and social issues as a result of their stature. However, the studies presented to the FDA proved only that the treatment achieved added one and one-half inches over the predicted height—none of the results of the study even attempted to show an effect on psychological and social well-being of the subjects. Despite discussion about the lack of impact on the subjects' psychosocial adjustment, the FDA was persuaded to approve treatment of healthy children without a medical condition.

Since FDA approval was obtained in 2003, thousands of healthy children have been subjected to hGH treatment. By prescribing hGH for healthy short children in an attempt to make them taller, doctors in effect are medicating healthy individuals to counteract a social prejudice, rather than as a response to a medical disorder. The proliferation of hGH treatment for children without diagnosable growth disorder shows that we as a society believe it is so bad to be short that we need to medically treat short stature even when it is not due to a real medical cause. While there are no data available that identify the exact proportion of children receiving hGH treatment who do or do not have a deficiency, a 2003 report suggested that about 40 percent of children on hGH therapy have no growth hormone deficiency.[16] Given the age of this report and the fact that the vast majority of extremely short stature has no medical cause, it is safe to assume that this percentage is probably much higher now. On July 23, 2014, the Partnership for Drug-Free Kids released a report on a study of 3,705 students stating that the use of hGH by teens had more than doubled in the previous year, with the number of high school teens in the study who used the therapy increasing from 5 percent in 2012 to 11 percent in 2013. The rate of use among African American and Hispanic teens was even higher, at 15 and 13 percent, respectively. The report did not distinguish between how much hGH was being used for the purpose of enhancing height and for another physical aspect. Nevertheless, this should be viewed as an alarming development. It received little attention in the media, and there has not been sufficient outcry from the medical community to draw attention to this problem.

No doubt this dramatic increase in availability and usage of hGH therapy is due in large part to effective marketing efforts by the pharmaceutical industry. Estimates in 2015 from the research firm GlobalData suggest that the global market for hGH treatment will continue to rise in value by 4.08 percent per year to reach $1.88 billion by 2024.[17] To promote more consumption, pharmaceutical companies are currently focusing on developing easier delivery options that would require only weekly or biweekly injections, rather than the current protocol of daily injections, which many patients find difficult. This change would require the drugs to be modified to be more long-acting, which no doubt will carry certain additional side effects yet to be explored.

## ETHICAL AND MORAL SHORTCOMINGS

The ethics of treating idiopathic short stature with hGH are more than a little questionable, on several grounds. Given how most children feel about examination of their genitals, being poked by needles, and staying overnight in a hospital, the intimidating and invasive testing protocol for a child who is healthy and normal is in itself traumatic. The testing should be reserved only for cases in which growth hormone deficiency is strongly suspected as a cause of the short stature. With only 5 percent of short stature resulting from real medical disorders, a better protocol is needed to determine who is an appropriate candidate for such testing.

To complicate matters further, as the supply of the hormone has increased since the mid-1980s, the number of children diagnosed with growth hormone deficiency has also mysteriously increased, to the point that it has become a fairly common diagnosis.[18] Unfortunately, there is no simple test that precisely and reliably detects growth hormone deficiency, because the human body secretes this hormone in bursts, making it difficult to measure with any certainty. As the body's growth hormone level rises and declines, much depends on when blood is drawn and how frequently. Several simultaneous tests are performed, and the results are often different, leading to interpretation issues and ambiguity. Furthermore, there is no consensus among doctors about which test values are the appropriate cutoff points for determining that a child has growth hormone deficiency.[19] As a result, some children who test with lower levels of growth hormone are labeled as having constitutional growth delay or familial short stature, while others with higher levels of the hormone are deemed to have growth hormone deficiency. These testing inconsistencies and the parental pressure exerted on doctors to give a satisfactory diagnosis have led to many normal children being misdiagnosed as having a growth hormone deficiency when they do not actually have one; some estimates are that as much as 70 percent of patients who are treated for growth hormone deficiency actually test normal after adolescence.[20] Because of the arbitrary nature of the definition of *growth hormone deficiency* and the poor reproducibility, sensitivity, and specificity of the tests, many patients currently labeled as deficient in growth hormone actually have normal levels of the hormone.[21]

Even when the testing reveals no hGH deficiency, many doctors still will prescribe hGH treatment. Such prescriptions are legal due to the FDA's approval of growth hormone use for idiopathic short stature. If we are determined to prescribe hGH treatment whether or not a growth deficiency is the cause of the short stature, why bother performing the testing at all? Why put the child through the experience and not just proceed with the treatment? The answer is that insurance companies will pay for the treatment if the diagnosis indicates a growth hormone deficiency. Without the diagnosis, most families would not be able to afford the treatment. Unfortunately, leading the parents and child to believe that the child has an illness or a defect in order to receive insurance coverage for hGH treatment is not only unethical and untruthful, but also harmful. It deprives the parents of the right to make an informed decision about the treatment and do what is in the child's best interest.

Once the parents decide to commence the hGH treatment, they are making a long-term commitment on behalf of their children. The treatment involves injecting a young child up to six days per week, amounting to over three hundred injections per year, over an average of six years but sometimes for as long as ten years. Studies have demonstrated that hGH treatment is statistically effective in that it enhances growth velocity and produces a final gain in height relative to pretreatment predicted height. However, there are three very critical caveats that are not fully appreciated by most parents who wish to start their children on this long-term treatment plan.

Caveat Number One: Immaterial Effectiveness    Repeated studies have shown that the treatment only increases the final height by an average of one or one and one-half inches, and sometimes as much as 2 inches, over the predicted adult height.[22] While that may be considered statistically significant by scientists, it really does not feel very satisfactory. After up to ten years of daily injections, a very short child can expect to become . . . a very short adult. So most children who were classified as having idiopathic short stature prior to receiving hGH treatment will be adults who will be classified as having idiopathic short stature after having received up to ten years of injections, except that they will be burdened with additional health risks as yet unknown and emotional suffering from having submitted to the treatment, both at a significant financial cost. Even with treatment, the person's adult height is still unlikely to be within the "normal" range. If a boy was predicted to reach five foot one in adult height without hGH treatment, how do we justify subjecting him to the trauma of invasive testing and daily injections for up to ten years only so that he might reach five foot two or five foot three?

The benefits of treatment are so limited that the treated individuals can expect to be subject to the same social bias after reaching their adult heights that they would have experienced without having endured the treatment. Sadly, many patients do not experience even such a small increase in ultimate height; only about half of the children who are not deficient in hGH have any response at all to hGH therapy.[23] There is wide variability among individuals treated. Coupled with the immaterial positive effect of hGH therapy, one must question whether practitioners should continue studying and promoting this treatment rather than educating parents about its futility and ineffectiveness.

Caveat Number Two: Faulty Foundation   The deemed success of the treatment is based on the difference between the *predicted* adult height calculated before treatment and the *achieved* adult height. This determination is based on an assumption that cannot be proved. Unfortunately, there is no foolproof, definite way to predict what a child's ultimate height will be prior to treatment. Some children who are slow to grow in childhood experience a big growth spurt in their late teens and eventually grow to be within the normal range. Some do not. Some children who have two short parents end up tall; some children who have two tall parents end up short. In addition, genetics, nutrition, unrelated illnesses, extreme stress, and growth delay are just some of the many factors other than parental height and bone measurements that may affect final adult height. Given all of these variables, accurate prediction is impossible.

To arrive at the predicted adult height measurement, scientists rely on some pseudo-scientific methods such as comparing X-rays of the child's hand and wrist with "standard" references and taking the midpoint of the parents' height and adjusting up or down based on the sex of the child. Doctors use these predictions to make critical and life-altering decisions. But these are not perfect predictors of what the child's adult height will be because the predictions are only 68 percent accurate and subject to large errors.[24] X-rays are easily misread or misinterpreted, and the prediction tables of "standard" references to which the child's readings are compared are derived from standards of hands only and not from any other areas of the skeleton. The predictive methods that doctors rely on today are more akin to consulting a crystal ball than science.

Furthermore, the magnitude of error can be as much as three or more inches. If the conclusion drawn from the studies is that hGH treatment offers an increase in height that is less than four inches greater than the predicted adult height, then such an increase is well within the margin of error. Since it is impossible to predict adult height within a credible level of precision, then the comparison between the predicted height and the achieved height is not very compelling. The claim that the treatment itself is effective falls within the margin of error and therefore is unreliable. The many testimonials of children who claim to have grown as much as eight or ten inches as a result of hGH treatment are highly suspect because there is no accurate method of predicting adult height. The child may have grown to that very same height with or without the treatment; no one will ever know.

Caveat Number Three: Where Is the Benefit?    The third caveat is perhaps the most puzzling. Presumably medications should be given to people based on a benefit that will be derived from them. The hGH treatment is advocated based on the assumption that short people suffer from psychological and social issues as a result of their stature. However, no one has proved that the treatment actually achieves any positive effect on the psychological and social well-being of the patients.

Many people believe that short people experience chronic stress and have significant problems with psychosocial adjustment and adaptation.[25] They presume that short children have lower self-esteem than children who are nearer average height, and that this effect increases during adolescence. They conclude that the experience of short children is so traumatic that treatment is justified even if it leads to only marginal, if any, increase in height. While they may be correct in their initial presumptions, at least with respect to some individuals, that does not mean that all short children suffer trauma as a result of their height, or that hGH is the appropriate answer. They make a logical mistake in assuming that the distress and social problems are caused by the short stature itself, rather than by the prejudice of others.

Medical professionals who treat short but healthy children with growth hormone do so based on a belief that it will bolster the child's confidence, but their decision is based on a feeling, not data. Without research and data supporting the assumptions that short stature causes psychological distress and social problems and that hGH therapy alleviates them, what we have is mere conjecture. Even assuming that short people do experience psychosocial problems, that does not mean that hGH therapy cures, or even allays, such problems, and logic would dictate that a mere one or two additional inches of height will not have a significant impact. Besides height, there are many other differences among children that also cause psychological distress and social problems, but the effects are usually temporary. It would be impossible to try to separate the stresses caused by height from stresses caused by other causes. Although anecdotally it is evident that short stature is a stressor, particularly in adolescence, very few adults have carried the rage they may have harbored as teens beyond those teen years. Furthermore, the social problems and distress that are caused by cultural prejudice should be addressed by using strategies intended to reduce or eliminate the prejudice, rather than by medical treatment of its victims.

When embarking on a long-term treatment designed to improve someone's quality of life, the most important consideration ought to be how the treatment itself will affect that person's quality of life. And yet not a single study demonstrates that hGH therapy provides any psychological or social benefit from the height gain. The FDA approved this treatment for short but otherwise healthy children without any data showing that the treatment made any difference in these children's lives; it was merely assumed that any additional height would correlate with improved quality of life. In fact, studies that tested this issue have shown that there is no significant difference in the quality of life between adults who had received hGH treatment as children and equally short adults who had not.[26] The only thing hGH therapy accomplishes is an additional inch or two of height (if one believes that the predicted adult height was accurate).

Even if we persist in believing that the benefits of treatment are worthwhile, we must first thoughtfully consider whether the benefits outweigh the risks of the treatment. Unfortunately, doctors typically minimize or gloss over the potential risks when they discuss hGH treatment with parents. They point to the fact that the FDA considers the treatment to be "acceptably safe." However, what we ought to be asking is whether any risk is acceptable when we start with a healthy patient, particularly a young child. And what amount of risk is permissible when there is no evidence of a material benefit?

The FDA cited a sixteen-year safety history of hGH treatment when it approved its use in children with idiopathic short stature. That determination was based on short-term data. Long-term effects were not available at the time of FDA approval. There have been many therapies that were considered safe initially but turned out to be dangerous. It took almost thirty years to discover that the cadaver-sourced hGH was contaminated with an incurable deadly disease. Cancer often takes a long time to develop and be detected. When considering whether to subject a young child who has not yet reached the age of consent to a long-term therapy, it is critical for parents to seek out enough information to become fully aware of the possible risks before embarking on such a journey. The risks are not immaterial, because the therapy involves introducing a healthy body to quantities of hormones that are significantly above normal concentrations. There has not been enough time and experience with this therapy to rule out the possibility of long-term side effects that are still unknown. However, some very serious risks of growth hormone therapy have been well-known for some time, and yet doctors rarely fully disclose them to parents and still subject healthy children to them. These known risks include the following:

*Stroke*: Children who receive growth hormone to treat short stature or hormone deficiency may be at increased risk of strokes as young adults.[27]

*Cancer*: Growth hormone causes the liver to increase the production of insulin-like growth factor (IGF-I), which is associated with a greater risk for prostate and breast cancer.[28] Also, several cases of leukemia have been reported in hormone-deficient children receiving hGH.

*Injections*: Some children receive over three hundred injections per year over the course of the treatment. Previous studies on children with diabetes have found that needles are one of the top stressors of their medical treatment.[29]

*Stigma*: hGH injections and the repeated examinations required as part of the treatment actually reinforce a negative self-image and the psychological issues that the treatment is designed to prevent. Further, there is no evidence that treatment improves depression or social adjustment issues that may have been present prior to treatment.[30]

*Renal effects*: hGH may aggravate preexisting kidney problems, potentially leading to kidney failure.[31]

*Metabolic changes*: hGH increases the metabolism, and some children may become unusually lean, losing body fat and becoming inappropriately muscular.[32]

*Other conditions*: hGH promotes development of conditions such as arthralgia and carpal tunnel syndrome.[33]

Numerous other bodily functions may be affected by hormones in ways that are not yet understood. Medical professionals and scientists are only beginning to learn about the interaction of different hormones and their impact on the systems of the body. Hormones are very powerful substances, and hormonal manipulation in general has consequences that medical professionals are just starting to discover and study, with their patients acting as guinea pigs. It is one thing to have adult patients voluntarily submit to being such guinea pigs; it is a completely different matter to subject young and healthy children to such experimentation.

The fact that only about half of hGH recipients respond in a statistically significant way to the treatment has led some in the medical profession to suggest that the therapy should begin earlier, before onset of puberty, and that both the dosage of hGH and the duration of the treatment should be increased. Since the FDA's approval, more and more children have been subjected to hGH, and hundreds of studies and experiments focusing on various aspects of these therapies have been conducted. The scariest part is that the safety of such higher doses and the long-term effects of hGH treatment in healthy individuals are completely unknown.

Subjecting young and healthy children below the age of consent, who do not have the ability to make their own decisions in medical matters, to such experimentation is not only questionable from an ethical stand-point, but one might even argue that it is a violation of the child's human dignity and right to be free of bodily torture. It may be understandable for parents to decide that their children should undergo an invasive, long-term therapy if they have a disease or medical condition that the treatment will alleviate, as long as the benefits are likely to outweigh the risks of the treatment. But treating healthy short children to modify their physical appearance in order to address a social prejudice does not pass ethical muster. Children as young as five years old have been involved in hGH therapy because doctors hypothesize that the treatment may be more effective when begun before bone epiphyses have fused. However, it cannot be known with any certainty that treatment of such young children is really effective, because the "success" of therapy is based on the child's predicted adult height: How accurate can such predictions be when considering a five-year-old for a therapy that will last for ten years or longer? By recommending hGH treatment for idiopathic short stature, doctors reinforce the message that taller is better—in fact, it is so important to be tall that we are willing to go to extremes to make children taller. Doing so sanctions prejudice against short people rather than alleviates it.

If doctors and parents view short stature as a problem to be fixed by medical treatment, what kind of self-image do we expect short children and adults to have? Rather than helping, this treatment reinforces the idea that short stature is a disability that warrants medical intervention. Rather than addressing the real cause—social prejudice—we have per-mitted healthy children to be subjected to medical engineering, turning the victim into a patient. It is society's prejudice that should be changed, rather than the victims of that prejudice. If there is no disease, there is no rationale for treatment. Just as it would never be considered ethically appropriate to systematically subject nonwhite children to skin-lightening treatments so that they avoid being subjected to racism, it should be considered equally unconscionable to subject short, healthy children to hGH treatment in an attempt to increase their height.

## HIGH COST OF TALLNESS

Another issue that must be considered is cost, which is estimated to be as high as $10,000 to $30,000 per year[34] for injections alone (not including office visits, lab tests, parental time away from work, and school absences). The actual cost depends on the size of the child—the larger the child, the more hormone he or she needs with each injection, leading to higher costs as the child grows. Of all children born in the United States each year, 90,000 will be below the third percentile for height. As an example, a single year's treatment of the 90,000 nine-year-olds below this height standard would cost upward of $2.7 billion. It is one of the most expensive treatments in our health-care system. Based on the average of six years of therapy, the cost amounts to about $30,000 for each centimeter of height. If a short person is lucky enough to achieve an optimistic outcome of an increase of six centimeters (about 2.3 inches) after having spent almost $200,000 over many years of treatment, that person would no doubt question whether this was the best use of that money. In a health-care system in which millions of people cannot even afford health-care insurance, how is this therapy justified for children who have no underlying medical disorder? What are the socioeconomic ramifications for the short children whose parents cannot afford to pay for such treatment? With the high rate of overdiagnosis of growth hormone deficiency, insurance companies usually foot most of the bill in those situations. Currently most insurance policies do not cover hGH treatment of idiopathic short stature, but if we continue to treat it as a medical condition, insurers will be pressured to begin paying for these treatments.[35] The likely result will be that these costs will be passed on to all of the insured and to employers through higher insurance premiums. Would not our limited health-care dollars be better spent addressing the many more serious diseases that currently have insufficient treatment options, rather than making short people taller?

## SHORT STORY

My own personal experience of going through these issues with my older son has been a perfect example of how this happens in real life and is what eventually led me to question and challenge these practices. I am four foot ten (and three-quarters), and my husband is average height, five foot ten. When our older son was born, he was exactly in the fiftieth percentile for both height and weight. I had received excellent prenatal care, and he was born a perfectly healthy and beautiful baby. During his first two years of life, we attended all of the required well-baby visits. Our pediatrician's office was a large practice, so usually we were seen by different nurses and doctors. His height measurements were all over the place, and it was not entirely clear where he fit on the growth chart. Because the percentile lines on the growth chart are so narrow, it appeared as though he was close enough to the fiftieth percentile curve, but sometimes the plotted points were on different lines. Thinking back, I recall how imprecise and informal the measurement taking was, conducted by different nurses, with little attention to precision. It was almost as if they needed to check the box and doing it correctly did not really matter. But back then we were completely uninformed about this issue and did not think anything of it.

Within his first few years of life, it became evident that my son's position on the growth chart had begun to slip toward the lower percentile curves. During each visit to the doctor, the first thing that was done was to measure his height and weight. Because he was always healthy, we did not have any other health concerns to discuss with his pediatrician, and his position on the growth chart became the focus of the doctor's visits. There really did not seem to be anything else going on at these visits besides taking the measurements, plotting the data on the growth chart, and administering vaccinations. It was almost as though plotting his growth was the primary purpose of the visit besides getting vaccinated.

Before he went to elementary school, my son was a very outgoing and social boy. He did not come across as shy or timid at all. He had no reluctance about approaching kids he had never met before on a playground, introducing himself, and joining in the play. By the time he was four, I started noticing that in the group pictures of his pre-K class he was at least a full head shorter than the other kids in his class. His height suddenly stood out as being something very different about him. I started paying more attention at his doctor's visits to his placement on the growth chart and asking the doctors more questions about it. By this point, his height was already below the lowest curve, with his percentile calculated at about–2.25 standard deviation, well below the third percentile. In other words, my four-year-old son's height was comparable to that of an average two-year-old boy.

The pediatrician ordered an X-ray of my son's hand and referred us to a pediatric endocrinologist at a large research hospital associated with a top private medical school in our state. At the time it was one of only two pediatric endocrinology practices in our city, and it took about six months to get an appointment. During the visit my son was measured with precise measuring equipment, with several measurements being taken. A physical exam revealed no abnormalities. We also had an interview about our family history, which covered the fact that he was born normal and all of his developmental landmarks were normal (he sat up, crawled, walked, and began speaking at typically normal times). He had no medical conditions, no allergies, and no history of malnutrition or other medical concerns.

After the visit we received a letter from the endocrinologist saying that his hand X-ray indicated that his growth was compatible with his age, which did not fit the pattern for constitutional delay. Because there was a lack of any apparent medical cause for his short stature, the diagnosis was idiopathic short stature. The doctor recommended that we bring him back in a few months to reevaluate his growth rate. She said that we had one or two years at the very most to wait before starting growth hormone treatment so that his height would be closer to his peers' during school years. She did not provide much information about what this meant or what our options were at that stage. However, she did say that the treatment offered only one or two inches of benefit, which was not much. She did not seem very forthcoming with information, and my perception was that given the absence of any underlying medical condition, she did not think it would be worthwhile for us to pursue hGH treatment. I had the sense that she was not interested in our case because there was no medical condition that needed attention.

We started measuring my son at home every few months and marking his progress on one of our bookshelves. He was not growing quickly, but he was growing consistently at about two or three inches per year. Having been short myself all my life, I did not want him to think that he was abnormal, and I was leery about embarking him on hormone therapy. However, I was beginning to feel guilty about being the parent whose genetic contribution was responsible for his short stature. I worried that he was the shortest kid in his school and that other kids would make fun of him. I started wondering why he was becoming less outgoing than he used to be and started connecting it to his height. By the time he was in elementary school, he was no longer the social, gregarious boy he had been; he was now more shy and quiet. He no longer felt comfortable approaching other kids on the playground and introducing himself. He kept safely to himself or with his existing friends, no longer inclined to proactively make new friends. He never voiced any concerns about his height, so we did not talk about it. We were careful about not making his height into a big deal. My husband and I figured that because he was a serious child, always excelling in school and sports, there was nothing wrong with his being a quiet person. We did not consider it a problem that needed correction. Although we tried to encourage him to be more socially outgoing, we did not press the issue when he refused.

At around age eight, he was still at least a full head shorter than all of his classmates but was still growing at a steady rate. He had continued to grow consistently at the same–2.25 standard deviation curve, below the lowest curve on the growth chart, and our pediatrician referred us to the pediatric endocrinologist once again for a follow-up evaluation. We decided to try another practice this time, hoping that a different doctor would be more forthcoming with information. At this visit, my son again was measured in detail. He also had a series of blood tests to evaluate his hormone levels and DNA for genetic disorders, as well as a full physical evaluation, including his genitalia. He was pretty shocked by this experience and looked like he felt humiliated. His sad face made me feel even more guilty for putting him through this ordeal, but I was hoping that maybe there was something out there that could make him taller. I was completely uninformed about issues that boys experience related to short stature, so I started doing some research on the Internet about growth hormones and began to think about his height more. I began to feel anxious about how difficult his life might be as an adult if he remained significantly shorter than other kids his age. Another X-ray of his hand was ordered.

Once again all the medical markers came back normal. All his hormones were normal; his chromosomal analysis showed no genetic abnormalities. His X-ray again showed that his wrist bones were compatible with his age. The doctor sat down and had a conversation with me to explain the process of measuring my son's growth hormone levels. I thought at the time that my son would not take it well. I expressed reservations that the testing process sounded scary and invasive and was unsure about the value of making my healthy son go through it. The doctor said that growth hormone treatment is expensive and the only way insurance would pay for it is to have the child go through the testing to attempt to produce results showing growth hormone deficiency. She made it sound as if there were ways she could help make it happen. She said absolutely nothing about the benefits or risks of the therapy itself, and I felt as if I were being gently encouraged to go forward with this protocol because my son's shortness was so severe. But the fact that he was healthy and that he had no underlying medical condition stopped me from moving forward. As a short person myself, I know that I would not want my stature to be considered a medical problem when it is not.

When I still did not consent to the testing, she suggested that as a first step, we should have my son eat a high-fat diet to see if a higher calorie intake might have a positive effect on his growth.

The high-fat diet did affect his growth, but only of his belly, not his stature. Several months after being on a high-fat diet my son was heavier, but no taller. We decided not to return to this doctor, because she had made us feel uncomfortable and pressured to pursue medical intervention that we believed to be unnecessary. But we continued to monitor our son's growth closely. As time went on, his growth rate did not change. He continued to go along the same growth trajectory, at two to three inches per year, but below the lowest curve on the growth chart. I decided to take one last chance and scheduled an appointment with yet another pediatric endocrinologist, really hoping for someone who would give me either peace of mind about pursuing further testing or reassurance that I had made the right decision by not pursuing growth hormone testing.

This time I was determined to see the leading expert in pediatric endocrinology in our state. This doctor was an older gentleman and a medical school professor. He reviewed my son's prior history, growth charts, X-rays, and records from the other visits to other pediatric endocrinologists. Then he had me measured as well. After reviewing all the data, he confirmed that my son had familial short stature and that he was perfectly healthy and normal. He said there was no way to know with any certainty how tall my son would be as an adult, but based on his experience, we could expect my son to reach an adult height of about five foot two.

I was a little shocked to hear this news, so I asked about growth hormone therapy. What little information that was available at the time on the Internet made it seem as though it was a good solution for any child who was very short, regardless of any underlying medical cause. I knew no details about it, but I could not understand what harm there would be in trying it out for a while to see if it might help my son grow taller. The doctor patiently explained how ineffective the therapy is for children who have been diagnosed with idiopathic short stature. He explained that the term simply meant that there was no known medical cause for it, but he assured me that my son was perfectly healthy and that his health record did not point to any evidence of growth hormone deficiency. He said flat out that the therapy was not worth the effort, discomfort, and expense for an extra one or two inches of height, and that the chances were pretty good that my son would not even gain that much height after several years of therapy. Even if he did, the small gain in height would not make any difference in his life, because he would still be considered extremely short. The doctor's explanation, tone, manner, and patience made me feel satisfied with the answers he gave me. He made me feel that there was nothing wrong with my son, and that there was no need to do anything about his height. After speaking with him, I felt that I could stop worrying about this issue. I came away from the visit assured that while my son might be short, he was perfectly healthy, and there was no need to continue pursuing the medical route to address whatever concerns might have remained.

Since then, I have resolved to help my son deal with his height by nonmedical means. His younger brother is also the shortest kid in his school and is following a similar growth pattern, although his deviation from the mean is slightly less severe. But I have not felt inclined to seek medical treatment for him. Like his older brother, he is short but otherwise perfectly healthy and normal. He is following his own growth curve. I have learned that I can do much more as a parent to help my sons cope with shortness by focusing on their character, teaching them to become more confident and resilient, and fighting against height prejudice in our society.

## A SUPERIOR SPECIMEN

The solution to prejudice is education for those who are its purveyors, not the genetic engineering of their victims.
ANDREW KIMBRELL, *THE HUMAN BODY SHOP*

The practice of weighing babies at birth began in the 1750s and makes perfect sense given the health risks faced by babies born with low birth weight. Lack of nutrition during pregnancy and infancy can have terrible effects that last throughout a person's life. It was not until the nineteenth century that measuring children's height was even considered a worthwhile endeavor. Francis Galton, a relative of Charles Darwin, was the first to promote this idea, with the goal of selective breeding for desirable genetic traits such as height. He was the person who coined the term *eugenics*.[36] This pseudo-scientific discipline became controversial and was abandoned after World War II, because it became associated with the Nazi pursuit of racial purity. Tallness was one of the admired virtues of the Aryan race. More recently, the pursuit of eugenics has been generally recognized as unethical and discriminatory.

Unfortunately we seem to have overlooked or ignored this understanding when it comes to height. Our current preoccupation with height measurement and the use of hGH therapy in healthy children are today's perpetuation of this immoral quest. In the United States thousands of children are currently receiving hGH treatment to "correct" their idiopathic short stature, at an enormous personal, social, and material cost and without clear evidence that such treatment provides a benefit that outweighs the risks. In essence, we are attempting to use medical intervention to physically alter an inherent trait that our society deems undesirable.

Doctors and clinicians must step back and reconsider their ethical obligations to these children. They need to be reminded of their ethical commitment to do no harm and to consider how their actions perpetuate the very social prejudice that they are purporting to treat. There is a lack of evidence that extremely short children with idiopathic short stature have any need for medical intervention. Medical professionals and pharmaceutical companies have generated an artificial demand for this product by creating unrealistic expectations on the part of parents that hGH treatment will be a magic solution to a perceived social problem. These elevated expectations often lead to disappointment, depression, and feelings of anger—the very psychosocial issues that the treatment was supposedly designed to address.

Treating children who may have had no significant underlying psychosocial issue may introduce anxiety or distress when the treatment does not meet expectations. Doctors would provide a far greater service by instead counseling and educating parents. Perhaps, rather than embarking on the testing and treatment practice, a referral to a psychologist would be the most appropriate action. Psychosocial adjustment issues should be addressed by psychosocial means, not by pumping hormones into children in a futile effort to make them grow. The person who experiences stigma resulting from short stature is better helped in other ways. Therapy and education would go much further than hGH treatment to help short children and their parents with anger and low self-esteem. The marginal effectiveness of the one and one-half inches of height gained through hGH treatment (if any is even gained) is not significant enough to address the issue of social bias against an individual who still will remain extremely short after the many years of treatment.

Doctors must be more alert to the stereotypes that they help to perpetuate by their incessant measuring, diagnosis of idiopathic short stature, and invasive and intimidating testing protocols, as well as to the ethics of using healthy children as guinea pigs in scientific experiments. Routine growth screening may be of value if it helps detect a medical condition, but given that such medical conditions are rare, pediatricians only heighten parental awareness and sensitivity to their children's stature and growth rates by making the measuring and charting of growth during office visits such a prominent event, as though it were the most important aspect of the child's health.

Treatment protocols communicate to children that something is so wrong with them that it justifies their being given daily injections for many years. The treatments serve only to reinforce the societal stereotypes about short people. Throughout the evaluation and testing process, doctors often fail to take sufficient care to reassure both the parents and the children that they are indeed healthy and normal, and that no medical treatment is needed. Instead, the doctors' belief that the short children will be socially and psychologically disadvantaged is often transmitted to the parents and the children.

Medical professionals need to stop treating short individuals as though they have a disease or a disability when they are healthy but happen to fall near the bottom of a "normal" statistical distribution.

Often it is not the doctors who advocate for hGH therapy; it is the parents. When parents bring a short child (most often a boy) to the pediatric endocrinologist for evaluation, they are typically worried that, being the shortest child in school, he will be teased for his shortness. They fear all kinds of other consequences: certain sports will be closed to him, dating will be difficult, he may have trouble finding a job as easily as his taller friends. Often the parents are themselves short, so their worries are understandable because they themselves have experienced the negative stereotypes and societal prejudice. They want to spare their child these problems. They have read about hGH therapy on the Internet and believe it to be safe and effective. They are eager to get him started on the treatment. They ask the doctor to prescribe hGH, and after some tests have been run to rule out a growth hormone deficiency, they refuse to accept no for an answer. They demand treatment and threaten to find another doctor who will comply with the request. Parents of short children may think that there is nothing wrong with hGH therapy for cosmetic purposes, that it is akin to a nose job or other medical treatments designed mostly for self-esteem or other psychological benefit. But these beliefs are mistaken.

In such instances, doctors have a responsibility to intervene if parents are making inappropriate decisions on behalf of their children. Young children have no understanding of what it really means to have daily shots for up to ten years or the possible side effects, which may not appear until many years later. Parents who make these decisions on behalf of their children often are more concerned about their children's height than the children are. Parents fret a lot about their children's short stature because of the parents' own preconceived social prejudice that taller people are more successful. They project these fears onto their children. These parents should not be permitted to make a decision to physically manipulate a child's appearance through an invasive, lengthy, and onerous medical intervention. Rather, they should be counseled about unknown risks involved in dumping extra hormone into an otherwise normal and healthy child. These risks may take years to discover. The parents should be educated that the evidence we do have thus far is that the treatment is not without potentially serious side effects. While some side effects may be acceptable to treat an actual medical condition, there is no justification to take such risks in the absence of a medical condition or real growth hormone deficiency.

Instead, parents should be encouraged to redirect their efforts toward teaching their children about acceptance of individual differences and valuing personal character. Parents should be educated on steps they can take to improve their children's adjustment to their height, because how children adapt to being short depends largely on the feedback they receive from their families. Yes, some short children experience teasing, but teasing happens for many reasons besides height, and very few are permanently scarred by it. Teasing is a normal childhood rite of passage and is not reserved for short children. In addition, hGH therapy is only marginally effective and quite variable, so it is unlikely that the therapy will do anything to improve their children's psychological and social adaptation. Most extremely short children who undergo hGH therapy still remain extremely short after treatment. It is not worth the potential health risks, enduring the discomforts and duration of treatment, or the cost.

### HIGHER VALUES

Parents of short children should feel free to rejoice in their kids' height instead of feeling sorry for them or medicating them. But until parents are liberated by social norms to do so, short children can learn to cope with social prejudice with the help of a supportive network of the adults in their lives. Parents, adult family members and friends, teachers, school administrators, and medical professionals such as doctors and nurses can help short children avoid and cope with issues like depression and low self-esteem. These problems are not exclusive to short children. Children are attuned to signals from their parents and will internalize any hint of anxiety or disappointment. If size is a focus of concern or strained whispers, children are likely to pick up on it and as a result may have lower self-esteem.

On the other hand, adults who are supportive will accept their children as they are and focus on their character rather than physical appearance. They work on cultivating coping skills in their children. Children with supportive parents tend to be more accepting of their bodies and more resilient. They tend to handle all types of adversity better. The best foundation for adjustment is to have good role models who promote positive self-image and self-worth. Children need to hear that their parents say they are perfect just the way they are. Sometimes it may seem to parents that they are unable to effectively help a child who may be having particular difficulty dealing with social stigma, and in those situations the child could benefit from receiving short-term counseling.

Awareness comes first. Although it may be natural for adults to treat short children as if they are younger than their chronological age, adults should take care to treat children according to their age, not their size. Resist the urge to juvenilize the smaller children (relate to them as if they were younger than their age), which may contribute to lower expectations of these children and immature reactions. Some may overcompensate by resorting to clowning or acting aggressively. To prevent such reactions, it is important that these children be treated based on their chronological age, rather than the age they appear. Make a conscious effort not to be overprotective. It is important that children learn to become more independent as they grow older, and their experience of their level of independence comes from comparison with other children of the same age.[37]

Parents can help relieve a child's anxiety by taking time to think before reacting. Too often parents' actions remind the child of who is bigger. Avoid resorting to affectionate diminutives such as "squirt," "little man," "kid," or "you're such a cute little girl/boy." Measuring children's height and marking it on a door frame will likely bring on more anxiety if the distance between marks appears too small. There is absolutely no need to obsessively gather this statistical information. No one cares.

There is no reason to believe that a short child is not as competent or intelligent as taller children or should shy away from sports. Short stature is not a handicap, and there have been many literary, musical, and historical figures who have achieved great success despite being short. One can find numerous examples of short people who have attained great accomplishments in all different kinds of endeavors. Quality of life and intellectual achievement are not causally related to stature.

Children should be encouraged to participate in sports, especially sports in which smaller size is either an advantage (gymnastics, wrestling, diving, equestrianship) or not a factor (golf, skiing, soccer). While taller people may have longer limbs, which may be an advantage in activities involving reaching, throwing, and jumping, they are more vulnerable to the impact of falls, because their taller bodies are less balanced and stable. A shorter person's smaller body generally has a lower center of gravity, which gives him or her an advantage in stability and makes him or her less susceptible to injuries. Even sports that have been conventionally reserved for the tall should not be ruled out, because there have been notable athletes of extremely short stature who have succeeded in all types of sports, including basketball (e.g., the five-foot-three Tyrone "Muggsy" Bogues). However, do not assume that sports have to be as important to the child as they are to you. Children may take an interest in sports and subsequently lose interest over time as they explore other activities. Participation in nonsport school activities and clubs is as effective as sports in instilling a sense of community and belonging.

When children encounter height discrimination, take advantage of the "teachable moments" just as you would when they encounter prejudice related to race, gender, or physical disabilities. Our society would benefit tremendously if all adults taught the children in their lives to appreciate their bodies just the way they are and to celebrate the diversity of the human race. Role-playing exercises can help children learn to cope with bullying, teasing, and name-calling. As stated before, bullying and teasing occur about all kinds of differences and are not exclusive to short stature, but size is one type of difference that really stands out.

For very minor incidents, adults should coach children to shake them off and act fearless in the face of a bully. Encourage children to use words to show that they have not been affected by the insult. Most of the time, bullies will never bother a child again if they see that the victim was not easily intimidated. If a child is feeling particularly upset, a good first thing to do is to acknowledge the unfairness of it, and that you realize that the experience is painful. But then point out that such setbacks are often temporary. Even with extremely short stature, there will come a point in every person's life when size will no longer be important, when height issues will no longer matter.

But when conflicts escalate into something more serious than just calling someone "shorty" or "fatso," parents and teachers should intercede rather than stand back and let the children "figure it out." Over the past two decades, our sensitivity to bullying has been heightened as a result of more than a few highly publicized incidents that led to fatal consequences, either suicide or homicide, including too many mass school shootings. These unfortunate events have shed a horrible light on the potentially extreme consequences of bullying, so it has now become unacceptable for parents, teachers, and school administrators to ignore such behavior.

While it may be natural for bigger children to dominate smaller ones even as young as preschool age, the adults are supposed to be there to help children learn what behavior is socially appropriate and what is not. The feelings of being an outsider, of being taunted and ignored, are painful memories that often last a lifetime; in the most severe cases, these feelings can grow into depression, hopelessness, and isolation. By interfering early and using the opportunity as a teachable moment, both the larger, more dominating child and the smaller or more timid child will learn the lesson that aggression is not a socially acceptable way to get what you want. Physical aggression may be a natural human instinct, but it can and should be unlearned as part of normal socialization. Adults must step in and intervene in bullying incidents, rather than ignore them and assume they are a harmless and ordinary part of childhood.

It is equally important to take the time to educate other adults who, although well-meaning, may say inappropriate things to short children. It is sometimes striking just how thoughtless some adults can be. For instance, teachers and gym coaches often line up the kids by height. Organizing kids by size seems an overly trivial way to achieve an appealing visual effect, but kids view it as a humiliating pecking order, and it is a source of many painful childhood memories for those who were at the undesirable end of the line. It raises awareness of the hierarchy of size, and the emphasis increases as kids get older and become more susceptible to stereotyping each other. Over time, it contributes to the erosion of the short kids' confidence.

The most important thing to keep in mind is that being teased is not a certain destiny for short children. Sure, many people want to be taller. But there is no need to assume that a short child is being bullied or that a child who is teased occasionally must be shy, moody, or permanently emotionally damaged by the experience. Do not fall into the trap that pharmaceutical companies have set in order to increase their profits. Sometimes our assumptions and gut feelings simply do not match the facts. Although short children are sometimes teased and tend to be treated as younger than their chronological age, this does not necessarily cause permanent social or emotional trauma for all of them.[38] Most short people overcome these difficulties and in the end are no different psychologically or socially than average or tall people.[39] Most short people learn effective coping mechanisms sooner or later.

On the whole, people tend to be quite hardy when facing adversity and do well as long as they have a supportive network of family and friends. Such a support network is crucial for all children regardless of size, gender, race, class, or physical ability in dealing with challenges of every kind and learning to overcome hardships that all people face in life. That is how we become stronger and more resilient human beings. Short stature is not a disability, but by confronting some of the difficulties related to short stature, an individual child can grow into a well-balanced adult who can competently handle all types of adversity.

The concern that dating may be difficult tends to be mostly related to short boys, rather than girls. Although women initially tend to prefer taller males, that does not preclude shorter men from dating and getting married. Yes, there are some superficial women out there, but there are plenty more women who do not care at all about height and just want to date someone who is a good person. Women who are so shallow that they place utmost significance on their partner's height are not worth dating anyway. As adults, we should encourage children—both male and female, short and tall—to develop an interesting and pleasant personality and good character, which are more constructive qualities for attracting a good mate than physical appearance. Most women would find a man who lacks confidence much less attractive than a man who is confident and short.

But to really address the underlying cause of the problem, we must do more than support our own children. We must work to end heightism in our culture. We owe it to our children, regardless of height, to provide an environment in which they feel that they belong and are unconditionally loved. Empower children to trust their own judgment and to believe in their own worth. Teach them to fight against social prejudices. We should focus our efforts on seeking greater acceptance of individual differences and emphasizing character rather than physical attributes.

# shortchanged in the workplace

IMAGINE THAT AN EMPLOYEE ARRIVES in his manager's office for his annual work performance evaluation and during the discussion, the boss states: "I was reluctant to hire you because, since you are Hispanic, I thought you were incapable." Regardless of what else she says during the rest of the meeting, it will be a tense and uncomfortable conversation. The employee will consider such a manager an adversary and will feel defensive and angry toward her in the future, and rightly so. No doubt after he reports this remark to human resources (HR), this manager will be reprimanded, perhaps even fired.

Now set that conversation aside. Instead, picture a work performance review, but the employee is a five-foot-three male, and the manager states: "I was reluctant to hire you because, since you are a little guy,

I thought you were incapable." The short-statured employee feels the same level of tension and anger toward the manager that the employee did in the other interview. However, after he reports this remark to HR, there are no consequences for the manager. HR tells the employee that there is no legal protection against what happened. Often it is the short employee who will face negative consequences from having reported the remark to HR. He might be labeled as overly sensitive, because after all, wasn't the manager actually complimenting him by telling him that he had overcome her initial presumptions? His manager might consider him insubordinate for having reported this event to HR.

Our social and cultural bias against short people is so profound that most people would not recognize anything wrong with the second example. Yet the second scenario actually happened to Chris Hamre, a five-foot-three, male employee working in a data entry job in New York City. What is it about a data entry job that this hiring manager could have considered too difficult for a person to perform simply because of his short stature? Should his height have mattered more if he happened to be in a professional position, such as an attorney, or in a manual job, such as construction?

Most people would assume that occupational success should be influenced solely or mostly by factors that directly contribute to performance, such as job-related competence, productivity, and intelligence. When pressed to think about it, we acknowledge that appearances do matter, and that attractive, well-dressed people are more likely to be successful, especially in appearance-focused occupations. However, we rarely consider how height is perceived and how much it influences workplace success, even for jobs in which appearance does not matter. Unfortunately, even though height does not affect how well workers perform their job duties, it is strongly correlated with both higher income and promotions to leadership roles. Most people would find it difficult to believe the extent to which an attribute like height, which is completely unrelated to job performance, plays a role in a performance-focused environment like the workplace.

Most short people find that their lack of height does not bother them very much until they are faced with workplace discrimination. There is no escaping the fact that height clearly matters in career success. It has long been recognized that short people face disadvantages in the workplace compared with their taller colleagues. John Kenneth Galbraith, an economist, described the favored treatment that tall people enjoy as one of the "most blatant and forgiven prejudices."[1] Height discrimination is as pervasive in the workplace as in the greater social world. It permeates employment decisions as much as race and gender do. In the workplace, taller people are more likely to occupy leadership and management positions and otherwise achieve higher status in professional and educational endeavors.[2]

From the very beginning of their careers and at each phase of their working lives, short people face prejudice. Many managers and coworkers instinctively consider short people less mature, less positive, less secure, less masculine (in the case of males), less successful, less capable, less confident, and less outgoing, as well as more inhibited, more timid, and more passive.[3] These are preconceived, superficial, and irrational judgments about a person's qualities—the embodiment of prejudice. Short people are presumed to possess these qualities before anyone takes the time to actually get to know them as individuals. People tend to be surprised when a short person is described as a brilliant or strategic leader. Short people who display confidence and leadership qualities are often referred to as "little dictators" or "little tyrants" in an attempt to belittle and minimize their influence.

To short people, the discussion of height in the workplace is particularly relevant and significant because it has a long-lasting material impact on their paychecks. But height discrimination in the workplace is no less relevant for the health of the workplace itself, and it should be as much a concern to executives as other forms of discrimination. The prejudice that contributes to unfair hiring and promotion practices, compensation discrepancies, and general failure to take short people seriously as individuals has led some of the most talented people to leave their jobs to pursue starting their own companies, which will often compete with their previous employers. Companies have much to gain from trying to keep these talented employees creating value for them rather than leaving to start a competing firm.

H. Ross Perot is a case in point.[4] The five-foot-five billionaire entrepreneur is intelligent, determined, and a consummate salesman. He initially joined IBM as a salesman and soon persuaded his manager to give him the most difficult customer accounts. During his stint at IBM, Perot made his sales quota every year, each year a little bit earlier. During his last year at IBM he reached his annual sales quota in the first three weeks of January. He repeatedly attempted to persuade his management to adopt his ideas, but they were rejected. Although he was the kind of man who could persuade even his toughest customers to listen to and agree with him, and his work performance, based on objective criteria of sales numbers, was superior to that of his colleagues, he could not convince his managers to take him seriously. He resigned from IBM and started his own company, EDS, with his own money. He later sold EDS to General Motors for $2.5 billion, started another company called Perot Systems, and later sold it to Dell for $3.9 billion. He also founded the Reform Party, ran for the U.S. presidency in 1992 and 1996, and is considered one of the most successful third-party political candidates in U.S. history. No doubt his former managers at IBM wish they had listened to him and done more to hang onto this talented man.

## GLASS CEILING IN A SKYSCRAPER

In all types of occupations, short people face difficulties in being hired as well as being promoted to higher level positions. Hiring managers usually will not admit that height is the reason for not hiring a candidate, but in fact it often is. Long ago, height often was considered explicitly in hiring decisions; a study in the late 1960s found that when job recruiters were given two résumés that were identical, but the candidates were different heights, the recruiters hired the taller person 72 percent of the time.[5] Today, even though height is rarely officially considered in hiring decisions, it remains an implicit factor in those decisions. A rational person might consider it reckless to exclude job candidates on grounds as specious as stature. Yet employers overwhelmingly believe that persons of above average height are more impressive to customers and are somehow more capable and competent. This occurs in both manual as well as professional occupations. Of course there is not a shred of evidence to support that assumption.

Most hiring managers who are interviewing candidates for a job are not even consciously aware that they are treating a taller candidate differently than a shorter candidate. But they must evaluate each candidate based in part on the perceptions that others, both inside and outside of the organization, would have of him or her, and inevitably height will affect those perceptions. How would a four-foot-ten sales rep, engineer, finance executive, or lawyer fit in with the rest of the team? How would such a short person interact with customers and other third parties? Often hiring managers have a difficult time envisioning such a short person on the board of directors or managing a multi-million-dollar customer account. Without overtly addressing the issue of height head-on, they conclude that the person is not commanding enough. The lack of physical impressiveness, or "presence," is painfully felt by both the candidate and the hiring manager. Think of all the value and talent that companies have missed out on by failing to consider shorter job candidates on such specious grounds, without ever giving the candidate an opportunity to prove his or her worth.

Even when they do manage to land a desired job, short people face a very low glass ceiling. Once on the job, their abilities are underestimated, and they are frequently overlooked for promotion to management and executive roles. There is a pattern that people in high-ranking positions are about two inches taller than those below them, even when comparing people of like educational and socioeconomic status.[6] In fact, the highest corporate ranks seem to be out of bounds altogether for short people, unless the short person's intellect or ability far outstrips his or her coworkers'. Rarely do short people manage to climb the corporate ranks to the top from lower levels within the organization. Their lack of "executive presence" makes executive positions literally out of reach. When we do find a short person as the head of a company or on the board of directors, it is usually someone who founded and built the company himself or herself.

As a four-foot-ten woman, I have enjoyed a twenty-year career as a corporate attorney. I consider myself to be a confident and determined person, one of the top performers at work. But it still took me almost a year, far longer than my classmates, to persuade a hiring manager to hire me for my first attorney job out of law school, even though I graduated with honors from a highly regarded private law school and had substantial job experience with excellent references. My first job was with a government agency, and I was the lowest paid of all my law school classmates, some of whose salaries were as much as two or three times more than mine. Since then I have managed to make some strategic moves so that my salary, while still lower than theirs, is now almost on a par with those of other lawyers of similar seniority and experience.

Despite my age, education, and career achievements, I still get teased about my height. The teasing usually is harmless, but depending on the context, it has been used in a disrespectful way to question my credibility or imply that I am too small to be taken seriously. One of my past managers had repeatedly teased me about my height in front of my coworkers and subordinates, which not only embarrassed me but had the effect of undermining my authority as a manager. In a professional role, the perception of authority sometimes matters more than anything else. I have also been passed over for promotions for reasons that were not well-articulated, having to do with others' perceptions of me and nothing to do with my qualifications or effectiveness.

My story is similar to the stories of many other short people who are confident, intelligent, and effective enough to achieve great career success but nevertheless remain stuck behind their equally confident, intelligent, and effective colleagues who just happen to be taller. We all have flaws, and one can easily say that it is those flaws, rather than our height, that are responsible for our lack of career success. It is easy to discount such testimonials as affecting only individuals, so statistical data can provide a broader picture. Recent research has confirmed that more than 90 percent of CEOs of large companies are not just overwhelmingly white and male, but also are well above average height. A majority of CEOs are three or more inches above average, falling within about the top 14 percent of the adult male population, and 30 percent of CEOs are at least six foot two, falling into the top 4 percent of the adult male population. Fewer than 3 percent of CEOs were below five foot seven.[7] Even in the presumably egalitarian environment of academia, assistant professors were found to be 1.24 inches taller, associate professors were 1.50 inches taller, professors were 1.97 inches taller, and department chairpersons were 2.14 inches taller than the average individual of their age and sex.[8]

The same effect is found among women executives. The few female CEOs of public companies are on average five foot nine, which is above the ninety-fifth percentile for women's height. Most people would presume that there might be a penalty on income for very tall women, because our cultural stereotype is that tall women are unfeminine. In fact, taller women have higher incomes than both shorter women and shorter men.[9] The taller the woman, the more likely she is to be promoted into management ranks, because she is perceived as more professional, dominant, and ambitious.[10] This lack of short people in the executive ranks of corporations, both male and female, demonstrates the existence of bias against short people in the same way that the absence of women and racial minorities in the executive ranks evidences bias against them.

One of my former employers is a typical U.S. multinational corporation that employs over 50,000 people. I worked at the corporate headquarters and had an opportunity to interact with a wide variety of employees throughout all of the departments in this company and at all levels of the organization, from administrative support up through management and the highest executive levels, all the way up to the CEO. In my time at this company I worked with people of all heights, from very short to very tall. There are some very short people in all types of departments throughout the organization. Without having done any statistical analysis, I have no doubt that if I plotted the heights of this company's employees, the chart would reflect a typical standard distribution curve.

However, not a single short person employed by this company is on the executive management team. While some short people have been promoted to middle management roles, none of the department heads, senior managers, business presidents, or vice presidents are short. In fact, at the highest executive levels, the closer the position is to the CEO, the taller the leader who occupies it. Although I do not know exactly how tall the CEO is, he is taller than all the executives who report to him. I observed the same phenomenon at all of my previous workplaces, which included other large companies, a university, and government agencies. While the executive leadership in the government agencies included more women and minority leaders, all of the women leaders, without exception, were unusually tall. Their heights were comparable to men's.

The discrepancy between the height distributions of the population of workers and the heights of corporate executives is striking. Why do we chalk up this fact to "that's life," when it is totally irrational? Height has become an attribute that is used as a barrier to exclude some of the best and most talented individuals from receiving the attention they deserve. Why is it acceptable for success to be conferred on one person based on such a meaningless advantage or to dismiss another person with potential because of the same meaningless attribute? Assuming that a company is staffed with people who fall into the standard distribution for height, one should expect that the height of individuals who are promoted into higher ranks will be similarly distributed. Short people should be in the executive pipeline along with taller people, so why should it be acceptable that the tallest people are promoted in such disproportionate numbers? It should not be unreasonable to expect employment outcomes, especially wages and promotions, to depend on factors related to productivity, leadership skills, education, and experience, rather than something as arbitrary as height.

## A SIZABLE WAGE GAP

Besides being more likely to be promoted, studies have shown that taller people make higher starting salaries and outearn short people throughout the duration of their careers.[11] One older study found that the starting salaries for tall men (six foot two and above) with MBAS was about 12.5

percent higher than graduates of the same school who were under six feet tall, even when the shorter man was considered more intelligent.[12] More recent studies have confirmed the existence of the link between height and wages, although the reasons for the relationship are still debated.[13] Two main hypotheses have emerged to attempt to explain why tall people are more successful and earn more in the workplace than short people: (1) that tall people have certain personal characteristics that help their on-the-job performance, such as self-confidence and better cognitive abilities, and (2) that short people face discrimination in the workplace due to cultural and social bias on the part of their managers.

An oft-quoted 2004 study delved into this issue by showing that income may be partly predicted by a person's height during adolescence, rather than the height ultimately attained as an adult,[14] speculating that it is confidence, rather than height, that leads to higher wages. The theory is that because of a lifetime of positive feedback, individuals who were taller as teens have been able to develop higher self-esteem and better self-image, leading them to participate in more social activities and pursue leadership roles in high school and college. By doing so, they are able to develop better interpersonal skills and confidence by the time they enter the workforce. The theory implies that it is those aspects of their personality and the variety of their social experiences during their teen years, rather than height itself, that contribute to their career success later in life.[15] On the other hand, the theory speculates that the stigma experienced by short teenagers and/or their lack of participation in groups leads to lower self-esteem and interpersonal problems that persist as they reach adulthood. Thus, the reason that certain workers make less money as adults is that their experience of being short has led them to become less easygoing and more risk averse.[16]

This theory, if true, highlights the long-lasting psychosocial effects of height discrimination experienced in adolescence and underscores the importance of addressing the social biases that our children experience as early as possible. However, the theory is not entirely convincing, because those characteristics that are deemed "higher self-esteem" and "better self-image" are based on nothing more than subjective perceptions that are associated with the inherent height bias that all people have (including the scientists conducting the research study). Designing and conducting a scientific study that effectively separates those perceptions based on stereotypes from actual personality characteristics would be difficult if not impossible. Moreover, the idea that short people are less successful and make less money because they lack confidence is an example of victim blaming. Short people do not cause height discrimination any more than racial minorities cause race discrimination or gay people cause homophobia.

Other researchers have concluded that the connection between height and workplace success is not affected so much by personality characteristics such as confidence, but instead, or in large part, by factors unrelated to job performance, such as employer bias.[17] This theory is more persuasive than the confidence theory, because it is supported by the fact that the same association between height and income/workplace success does not exist for individuals who are self-employed and who therefore are not subordinate to employers.[18] This fact alone confirms that the height wage gap in the workplace is more a result of bias on the part of managers, rather than of any incompetence, lack of self-esteem, or other shortcoming on the part of employees. Even considering that lack of confidence may be partly responsible for some of the wage gap, the bottom line is that the height wage gap exists, and it cannot be explained away by reasons that do not include at least some level of bias or discrimination.[19]

Regardless of the root cause, the impact on wages and workplace success for short workers is alarming. Despite the hypotheses that try to explain the reasons for the wage gap, the fact remains that there is a considerable association between height and wages. Disparities in pay for short people are similar to race and gender wage gaps. Because height is as easy to observe as race or gender, the similarity is not surprising. In one oft-cited study,[20] researchers found that taller people earn about 1.6–2.2 percent more per inch of height per year than shorter people. Thus, an average worker earns approximately $789 more per year for every inch of height. Among male workers, the tallest quartile earned

13 percent more than the shortest quartile. For example, a man who is six feet tall but who is otherwise identical to someone who is five foot five would make on average $5,525 more per year, even after controlling for other factors such as gender, weight, and age. In other words, this differential is based solely on height alone.

Is it possible that taller people actually perform better on the job than shorter people? A few studies have been done on salespeople, whose success can be evaluated based on more objective performance criteria (such as sales volume) than other professions. There is a widespread assumption that tall salespeople sell more than short ones. However, sales figures have not borne out this belief.[21] Sales performance is actually related to submission, not dominance, and as a result, average or shorter salespeople are actually more successful in sales than tall people, who may be viewed as overbearing. Managers nevertheless prefer to hire tall employees for sales roles, mistakenly believing that their height will impress customers. In fact, their height intimidates customers.

Logically, any relationship between height and income should disappear once managers have the opportunity to observe the performance of their employees. Even if height has some advantageous effects on income at the start of one's career, they should dissipate over time, as the shorter person proves his or her worth and performance. Unfortunately, once on the job a short person who performs well is still often deemed less capable than a taller colleague, because a manager's evaluation of an individual's job performance is colored by bias. During performance reviews, managers assess both objective and subjective factors. Objective factors are those measurable aspects of performance, such as outcomes and results (who generates the greatest sales volumes, who received the most favorable customer reactions, etc.). Subjective factors, on the other hand, are those based on perceptions, such as how the manager and others value the employee. These subjective factors are very susceptible to bias. Inevitably, subjective evaluations will color how a manager evaluates even the objective factors. Managers tend to assume that customers will admire and respect a tall person and be more likely to buy from a tall person. They may further assume that a tall person who is so admired will be more able to develop trust, acquire information, or negotiate more effectively. These biases affect that manager's subjective job evaluation even if there is no objective basis for these assumptions, and even when the objective performance results do not support the assumptions.[22]

Furthermore, if due to the manager's bias the manager provides the tall salesperson with the better sales leads, that results in a self-fulfilling process that makes it appear as though the manager's biased assumptions were correct. Thus, height affects performance evaluations twice: managers' subjective performance ratings are based in part on actual performance and in part on self-fulfilling processes whereby managers are more likely to attribute greater performance to taller people. This has a direct and detrimental impact on the professional success of short people at work and explains why so few ever get promoted to executive levels where they will make higher salaries. The bias may be subtle, and no doubt most managers do not even think that prejudice motivated their decisions, but the impact is inescapable and not insignificant. The manager's bias distorts how shorter employees are rewarded compared to taller employees, leading to fewer promotions and lower pay for short people. This same bias is at work not just in sales roles, but in all types of occupations.

Consequently, although one would hope that the pay gap would disappear after a manager has an opportunity to get to know a short employee, data show the opposite result. In fact, the disparity in income actually increases over time. Height becomes more and more positively correlated to income over a person's career at all levels of employment, from leadership to management, and on down the corporate ladder, suggesting that discrimination faced by short workers continues to persist despite ample opportunities for their managers to assess their level of skill and competence.[23] One study found that about 15 percent of the height wage premium is explained by selection into managerial positions.[24]

## WAGE GAPS: HEIGHT VERSUS GENDER VERSUS RACE

Both the race wage gap and gender wage gap are well known and accepted as fact. While some may debate the size of these gaps, many studies have demonstrated that there is a significant difference in pay between men and women and between white and nonwhite workers, even when controlling for other factors. Actually, there may be an interesting interplay between the gender wage gap and the height wage gap. As mentioned in chapter 1, when assessing the relative stature of another person, it usually takes a difference of about five inches or more for someone to perceive that the other person is much shorter or taller. Given that women are on average about five to six inches shorter than men, and shorter men have the same wage gap to taller men, it is possible that the gender wage gap is a factor of the height differences between men and women. Perhaps what we sometimes tend to assume is sex discrimination is actually height discrimination. More likely, both types of discrimination are independent of each other and both have a significant impact on wages.

Because none of the studies published to date have attempted to evaluate the effect of the height wage gap over time, nor have they delved into the interplay among the gender wage gap, the race wage gap, and the height wage gap, I decided to conduct an informal study of my own, following the methodology described in a paper published by Stephen Brown.[25] The U.S. government makes available vast amounts of data that can be analyzed by anyone with some patience and a little bit of knowledge. The U.S. Bureau of Labor Statistics maintains databases that include many years of data on workers and contain information about a variety of their personal characteristics, such as occupation, age, race, gender, height, and income. The most recent survey included in the database was begun in 1997 and had almost nine thousand respondents born between 1980 and 1984. They have been interviewed annually since their original enrollment. This allows for a comparison of their wages over time as they have progressed in their careers.

Based on the data set from the 1997 survey, 4,599 (51 percent) of the respondents were male and 4,385 (49 percent) were female. In addition, 4,665 (51.9 percent) of the respondents were white/non-Hispanic, 2,335 (26 percent) were black, 1,901 (21.2 percent) were Hispanic, and 83 (0.9 percent) were of mixed race. For the purpose of my informal study, I combined Hispanic, black, and mixed-race respondents together into a "nonwhite" category in order to compare the race wage gap based on white versus nonwhite, rather than attempting to probe further into individual racial differences.

To ascertain the impact on wages as people progress through their careers, data were compared from the years 2000 (when the respondents were at the beginning of their careers) and the latest data set available, year 2011 (when the respondents had been in the workforce for about a decade). (The relevant data can be retrieved via the NLS Investigator tool provided by the Bureau of Labor Statistics Web site, at https://www .nlsinfo.org/investigator.) After collecting the relevant data points, Excel and Mathematica programs were used to compare the incomes of people by gender and height and also by race and height.

Gender versus Height    The data show that regardless of gender, taller workers make more money. The results of the analysis confirmed that tall people of either gender earn higher incomes than short people, and that the wage gap widens over the course of their careers. In the year 2000, when the respondents had just entered the labor force, there was a slight height wage gap for both genders, but it was more noticeable among women, with taller women earning substantially more than shorter women. The gender wage gap was actually the opposite of societal assumptions, with taller women outearning men (including taller men).

However, this phenomenon was reversed after ten years into the respondents' careers. Comparing the data from 2011, there was a significant gender wage gap and an even more significant widening of the wage gaps for both gender and height. By 2011 men clearly outearned women regardless of height. Also, the height wage gap grew for both men and women, with tall people of both genders earning substantially more money than short people of both genders. By the time workers have been in the labor force for a significant period of time, acquiring both experience and relationships, the wage disparity is even more striking, with the premium for height approximately 3.5 percent per inch (or over $2,000 per inch) for men and 2.5 percent per inch (or $1,000 per inch) for women. This shows that the previous studies done on this subject were not nearly detailed enough, because they averaged all incomes of all workers together to get a single snapshot at one point in time. In fact, the wage gap increases over time, and we can expect that as workers progress further in their careers, the wage gap becomes much more serious than is shown by the general point-in-time income information that has been published to date. Assuming that the trajectories will continue at this rate, over a person's thirty- or forty-year career, the wage gaps for both height and gender would be far greater than previously presumed.

Furthermore, the way the lines diverge suggests that height plays an even more important role than gender in people's incomes, because the wage difference is much smaller between short men and short women than between tall men and tall women. In addition, the two graphs in chart 3 suggest that height has a bigger impact on men's income than on women's, because the line depicting men's income rises much more steeply as the individual's height increases. What is most interesting about the data is that one is able to see a comparison of wages earned by the same individuals over time. While the respondents all started off their careers earning relatively similar wages, during the subsequent ten years the shortest individuals' wages approximately doubled, while the tallest individuals' wages almost tripled. The particular cause would be difficult to discern—it could be discrimination or it could be the result of individuals' career choices (some of which could be influenced by discrimination)—but the correlation is troubling nonetheless.

Race versus Height   A similar analysis was conducted comparing income affected by race and height over time. As with gender, taller workers made more money, regardless of race. At the beginning of the respondents' careers, while there was only a little income difference between short nonwhites and tall nonwhites, there was a substantial height wage gap among white respondents.

As with gender, over the course of ten years both wage gaps widened dramatically. By 2011 white respondents outearned nonwhites by an average of $7,500 per year. The graphs in chart 4 also show that a sig-

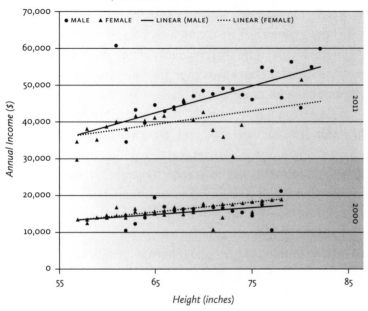

CHART 3 Income versus Height on the Basis of Gender, 2000 and 2011

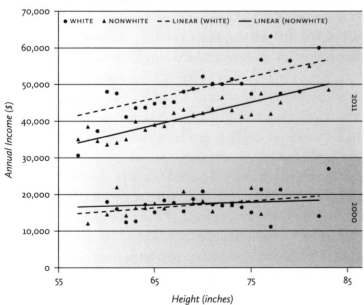

CHART 4 Income versus Height on the Basis of Race, 2000 and 2011

nificant height gap affects both whites and nonwhites in a similar way. Based on this data set, average income for whites increases by $585 for every inch of height and for nonwhites by $616 for every inch of height. Unlike the gender graphs in chart 3, which showed that height affected men's income somewhat more than women's, the 2011 lines in the race graph appear more parallel to each other, implying that height affects whites and nonwhites in a similar way.

The influence of height on income is clearly evident in both cases analyzed above and affects income separately from and in addition to both gender and race. However, the analysis also reveals that the relationship between height and income is not a simple, linear one. There are some plot points on each graph that depart from the trend lines. This occurs because some individuals at the bottom and top of the height range had income outside the regression line.

Obviously there are many factors that influence an individual's income besides height, such as education level, industry, and occupation. These factors also affect the linear regressions depicting the gender wage gap and the race wage gap. Unfortunately, none of the studies published to date has explored income differences based on height within a particular occupation or industry, and the data sets maintained by the Bureau of Labor Statistics do not provide a sufficient sample size to evaluate the effects of height on wages among people in a single occupation. Hopefully someone with a scientific background and sufficient funding may take up a research study to evaluate this in the future. To try to shed some light on this issue, the existing data set was used to compare individuals in four occupational sectors: manufacturing, construction, retail, and education and health. The results confirm that the impact that height has on wages depends to a large extent on the industry in which the person works.

The data depicted in chart 5 show no height gap at all within the retail and education and health sectors. That means that there is no height premium among respondents who work in these sectors, at least when viewed at one point in time (the effect of height over time within these sectors was not studied). On the other hand, the manufacturing and

CHART 5  Income versus Height
on the Basis of Occupational Sector

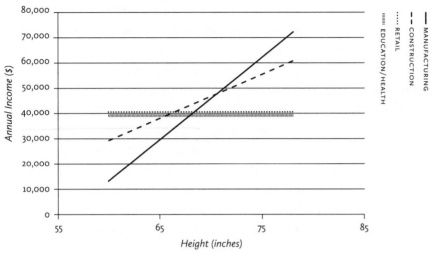

construction sectors depict a vast height wage gap, showing average annual income increases of $3,200 and $1,750, respectively, for every inch of
height. Furthermore, the relationship between height and wages in these
two sectors is a simple linear relationship. This glaring discrepancy is no
doubt responsible for the absence of a simple linear relationship between
height and wages when looking at all workers together as a group, rather
than at specific industries. The graph in chart 5 clearly demonstrates that
workers in some sectors do not suffer the same extreme levels of height
prejudice that workers in other sectors do.

It may appear logical to accept such an extreme wage gap in the manufacturing and construction sectors because traditionally manual labor
jobs have placed a high value on physical size. However, the severe slopes
of the lines in these two sectors suggest that something else is at play
besides a simple preference for physical size. The higher wage range
($60,000–$80,000) is more likely to represent managers, who are all
on the tall end of the graph, while the lower wage range on the bottom
of the line ($20,000–$40,000) represents income of the manual labor
workers, who are much shorter. While it may be understandable that

an extremely short person seeking a manufacturing or construction job may not have the physical strength or reach that a very tall person might have (although there are many short people who are very strong), the lower wages for the shorter workers indicate that they are the ones occupying the manual labor jobs, while the taller respondents have the management jobs. Assuming that short people would be as effective in management roles as tall people, but perhaps less effective at manual labor jobs than tall people, one would actually expect that the line would slope the other way: that taller people would have the lower-paying manual labor jobs. This graph represents the opposite effect.

Moreover, even looking at the slope as it affects the tallest individuals, why should someone who is six foot five earn an average of almost $10,000 more than someone who is six foot two? Both individuals are objectively very tall, and the three-inch height variance between them should make no difference whatsoever, even in the most physically demanding jobs. Further examination of the vast wage gap in the manufacturing and construction sectors points to the existence of severe height discrimination in those sectors.

Nevertheless, while height discrimination in the workplace may be more or less severe depending on the worker's occupation and industry, as depicted by the wage analysis above, I contend that height discrimination still exists in every occupation and in every sector. It affects individuals in ways that may be large or small, obvious or subtle. While height may not appear to affect income when analyzing a particular sector such as education at a single point in time, that does not mean that there is no height wage gap over the course of a person's career in that sector. Given managers' inherent biases, it is inevitable that even in the most egalitarian sectors, like education and government, where employees earn a predetermined salary based on their position and years of service, height eventually will have an impact on their ability to be promoted to management and executive roles, which are accompanied by higher income. Height also affects careers in professional occupations in areas such as academia, finance, medicine, and law, although the effects are more subtle than they are in the manufacturing and construction sectors. Women and minorities have to overcome great obstacles to approach the corporate glass ceiling, and few have managed to break through it. Height adds an even greater obstacle to the mix and makes that glass ceiling even more impenetrable.

The key to ending all types of wage gaps is transparency about compensation. Making salaries public information will quickly shed light on any pay disparities in an organization. Transparency also would help address whether employees' feelings of injustice are real or merely perceived (i.e., are not supported by the facts). If the pay disparity is real and cannot be explained by objective criteria such as experience and education, then in order to retain talent, organizations will be forced to make corrections. Transparency is the necessary element to ensure that workers receive equal pay and that any inequalities are explained by valid and rational reasons unrelated to bias.

## LEGAL LIMITATIONS

There are many countries in which height discrimination is not only acceptable but actively sanctioned. For example, Russia recently passed a law that prohibits short people under four foot eleven from driving,[26] an otherwise normal life activity that short people capably perform everywhere else in the world. In China and many other Asian countries, height requirements are routinely specified for jobs, including government jobs, that seem to have no need for them.[27] Positions that frequently impose a height requirement are as routine as cashiers, receptionists, bank tellers, and many other occupations for which height should be irrelevant.

In many Asian countries taller workers performing identical work often earn more. In the October 25, 2014, issue of *The Economist,* about China, it was reported that a guard who was only two inches taller than his coworker earned a larger paycheck "because bigger guards make people feel safer." But even ads for positions such as hotel cleaning staff often impose a minimum height, often requiring women to be at least five foot four. In a country where the average female is five foot two, it makes no sense that a cleaning woman should have to be especially tall. Furthermore, even in other occupations, the higher the rank of the position, the taller the stature that is required, according to a November 15, 2015, issue of *Foreign Affairs;* one employment ad from a restaurant in southwestern China required a female kitchen aid to be at least four foot nine, a waitress to be at least five feet, and a hostess to be at least five foot five. It is common in China that jobs with different status are associated with people of different heights, and candidates are often rejected for jobs explicitly for being too short. While some lawsuits have been filed, including against government agencies that have discriminated against shorter workers, courts have thus far refused to consider them.

The state of affairs is similar in other Asian countries, such as South Korea, the Philippines, Thailand, and India. Even Western companies operating in Asia fall prey to the same practices: a recent employment ad for Ace Hardware in the Philippines advertised that cashiers must be at least five foot two and utility clerks must be at least five foot six (which is exceedingly tall for a country where the average man is five foot four and the average woman is four foot eleven). It seems that height is an even bigger an obsession in Asian countries than it is in the United States. Throughout Asia, and wherever in the world height has acquired preeminence, the consequences are heart wrenching: the number of limb-lengthening surgeries performed in countries like Russia and throughout Asia is far higher than in the rest of the world.

In the United States most employers no longer impose physical requirements, but workplace height discrimination, while not as overt as it is in Asian countries, remains a fact of life. Federal antidiscrimination laws were enacted to protect individuals who fall into certain legally protected categories. Under Title VII of the Civil Rights Act of 1964, it is illegal to discriminate against people on the basis of race, color, religion, sex, and national origin. There are also federal laws prohibiting discrimination based on age and disability. These laws were enacted because historically, individuals who fall in these categories have experienced societal prejudice that affects their ability to be hired, be promoted, and receive equal pay. However, despite the fact that short individuals also experience societal prejudice that affects their ability to be hired, be promoted, and receive equal pay, workplace height discrimination remains legal under federal law.

Thus far, efforts to extend legal protections to cover height have not been successful at the federal level, but there are a handful of local laws in various parts of the country that specifically protect individuals against height discrimination. Michigan is currently the only state that prohibits height discrimination, with similar legislation having failed to pass in Massachusetts and Utah. A few cities have passed ordinances to address this issue: Santa Cruz and San Francisco, both in California, are two municipalities that have ordinances prohibiting height discrimination. The District of Columbia prohibits discrimination based on personal appearance, which includes height among other characteristics. Outside of the United States, there are similar laws in Ontario, Canada, and Victoria, Australia. Outside this handful of geographic areas, height discrimination is considered legal.

Despite study after study proving that short people experience societal prejudice that affects their ability to be hired and promoted at work and receive less pay than taller people, most people generally do not think of height when it comes to antidiscrimination laws. One of the reasons for this is that victims typically do not even realize that their managers' behavior is motivated by height bias. Height discrimination is largely unrecognized, and even short people themselves rarely realize that their lack of workplace success may be the result of heightism.

Nevertheless, in certain limited circumstances existing federal antidiscrimination laws have been used to dispute employment practices that disproportionately affected short workers because of their membership in a legally protected group. The following discussion illuminates this principle, pointing out its significant limitations.

Title VII    To win an employment discrimination case under Title VII of the Civil Rights Act of 1964, the employee must show that either (1) a neutral employment practice negatively and disproportionately affected a protected group, or (2) the employer was motivated by discrimination in treating the employee less favorably because of his or her membership in a protected group.

In the context of height discrimination, the first theory usually involves the use of minimum height restrictions. Some short employees have been successful when they proved that an employer's minimum height restriction had an adverse impact on women and certain racial and ethnic groups. In the 1970s a series of court rulings found that employers discriminated against women by assuming that height was necessary where strength was deemed essential to job performance. These decisions led to an end to most height requirements for public positions such as police officers and firefighters.[28]

In the precedent-setting 1977 case *Dothard v. Rawlinson,* the U.S. Supreme Court found that an Alabama law that required prison guards to be at least five foot two and weigh 120 pounds violated Title VII because it would exclude 41 percent of the female population while excluding less than 1 percent of the male population. Likewise, in *League of United Latin American Citizens v. City of Santa Ana* (1976),[29] the California District Court determined that the city's minimum height requirement for police and fire departments disqualified two to three times as many Mexican American applicants as Caucasian applicants. And in *Sondel v. Northwest Airlines* (1993),[30] the EEOC found that the airline's five foot two minimum height requirement for flight attendants discriminated against women, especially Asian and Hispanic women, in employment opportunities.

A potential avenue to address workplace height discrimination against short men and tall women is the theory of gender stereotyping. Under this theory, the argument is that discrimination against short men is based on the social bias that short men lack the physical height and strength expected of a man and are therefore unmanly. Likewise, women who are tall may be perceived negatively for defying the societal expectation that women should be demure and feminine. This theory has been used successfully in discrimination cases involving sexual orientation, which also is not protected under Title VII. For example, in *Nichols v. Azteca Restaurant Enterprises, Inc.* (1979),[31] the court found the employer's actions were linked to gender because they reflected the employer's belief that the homosexual employee did not act as a man should act. This theory might be similarly used by a short man to claim discrimination based on gender stereotyping because his short stature is perceived to be unmanly. Unfortunately there have not been any cases yet to test the effectiveness of this theory. Prevailing in such a Title VII case will be more likely if the short man is able to show that all short men working for the same employer receive lower wages than similarly qualified taller employees.

Overall, Title VII has been a poor vehicle for pursuing height discrimination cases, except in a very few limited circumstances. Lawsuits that have attempted to use the second theory, namely, that an employer treated an employee less favorably because the employer was motivated by discrimination, have usually been unsuccessful. In those lawsuits, if evidence is lacking or the discrimination appears to be based more on height than on gender or some other protected trait, the courts tend to rule against the plaintiff, because Title VII does not prohibit height discrimination. Victims of employment decisions based on height discrimination often have a difficult time gathering enough evidence to prove that the employer's motive was based on a legally protected group, not on height alone. This leaves short employees who may have been repeatedly denied promotions and subjected to teasing and bullying with no way to pursue a legal claim based on Title VII.

Americans with Disabilities Act   An avenue that may be available to extremely short employees is based on the Americans with Disabilities Act of 1990 (ADA), which prohibits discrimination based on disability.[32] Under this law, the plaintiff must first establish a disability, which is defined as "a physical or mental impairment that substantially limits one or more of the major life activities" or "being *regarded as* having such an impairment." A short person who is short due to a medical condition is usually in the best position to pursue an ADA claim based on the condition. However, given that only about 5 percent of extremely short stature is caused by a medical condition, most people who are extremely short are physically healthy and typically cannot successfully pursue an ADA claim based on their height as a disability, even if they are no taller than another worker whose short stature is caused by a medical condition.

Another hurdle the employee would have in pursuing an ADA impairment claim is establishing that the impairment substantially limits a major life activity. Thus far, courts have rejected ADA claims absent a medical condition for short stature, finding that height alone is not a disability because it does not substantially limit an individual's ability to engage in a major life activity. The law codifies a nonexhaustive list of qualifying life activities, including "caring for oneself, performing manual tasks, seeing, hearing, eating, sleeping, walking, standing, lifting, bending, speaking, breathing, learning, reading, concentrating, thinking, communicating, and working." The law further states that an impairment need only limit one such activity to render someone "disabled." Of course simply being short, without an underlying physiological impairment, usually does not limit one's ability to engage in any of the listed activities. However, the list of qualifying major life activities is not comprehensive and may be interpreted in the future to include activities that short stature does substantially limit.

In one recent case, *McElmurry v. Arizona Department of Agriculture* (2013),[33] a plaintiff attempted to raise such an argument. The court acknowledged that short stature could in some contexts substantially limit one or more of the major life activities of an individual and that a normal physical characteristic such as short stature can become a protected disability if it falls outside the normal range. Unfortunately the claim subsequently was dismissed without analysis of this issue, because the employer, a state agency, enjoys governmental immunity from suits based on the ADA.[34] To date, no court has considered this issue on its merits, but the *McElmurry* opinion has opened the door for this issue to be interpreted less restrictively in the future than it has been so far.

It is theoretically possible for the ADA to be used to pursue a claim that is not based on impairment. In interpreting the ADA, the Equal Employment Opportunity Commission (EEOC) has promulgated regulations[35] that go so far as to suggest that short stature that is not the result of a medical condition might be the subject of a viable ADA claim even if it does not rise to the level of an impairment, as long as the deviation in height is outside of the "normal" range. The "normal range" claim is a potential avenue that is available to individuals whose extremely short stature has no medical cause. Thus far courts have not read the regulations to allow ADA protection for short stature absent a physiological disorder. But based on the plain reading of the regulations themselves, it is evident that courts have construed the regulations too narrowly and failed to even consider the "normal range" provision.

The term *normal range* is not specifically defined in the EEOC regulations or interpretive documents, so medically healthy but short individuals would have to overcome the hurdle of proving just how extreme the deviation in height must be to qualify as impairment. The determination of what falls within the "normal range" seems arbitrary. The most convincing argument may be to look to statistical standard deviation. Statisticians and a majority of medical sources generally consider the shortest 2.5 percent and tallest 2.5 percent of the population to be outside the "normal range." A 2.5 percentile benchmark also compares favorably with other regulatory benchmarks for height, such as FDA regulations. Based on the most recent data collected by the National Center for Health Statistics, men shorter than five foot four and women shorter than four foot eleven would fall outside such a "normal range."

There is one more avenue that may be available to short individuals besides proving that they have a disability that substantially limits a major life activity. That is the "being regarded as impaired" theory, which protects a person if an employer discriminates "because of an actual *or perceived* physical or mental impairment *whether or not the impairment limits or is perceived to limit a major life activity*" (emphasis added). Regardless of whether or not extremely short stature is an actual physical disability, it is certainly viewed as inferior in our society, as evidenced by the widespread use of prescription hGH therapy for short but physically healthy children. A case based on the perception of impairment, rather than actual impairment, may be viable.

It is important to note that under the "regarded as" theory, it is unnecessary to prove whether a person's height is at or below the "normal range," as long as the employer regards the person's short stature as an impairment. In a "regarded as" claim, the question is whether an employee's actual or perceived impairment motivated an employer's adverse employment action. The "regarded as" theory does not apply to minor impairments that are expected to last six months or less and does not require employers to provide reasonable accommodations or modifications to such employees. This theory has not been used in height discrimination cases yet, but it may be an important potential avenue for pursuing cases involving failure to hire or promote or disparate wages.

The theories presented in this section are mere speculations about how a short worker might pursue an employment claim based on height discrimination. To date, no such claims have been successfully prosecuted. The prospects of successfully bringing a workplace discrimination claim based on height are bleak because federal antidiscrimination laws are intentionally silent about height. But even in jurisdictions that do have laws prohibiting height discrimination, few cases have been brought. In Michigan, the only U.S. state that prohibits height discrimination, lawsuits based on height have been exceedingly rare even though the protection was added to the law in 1976. The only publicized height discrimination lawsuit in Michigan settled out of court. The 2014 case was filed by a four-foot-seven woman who had been hired as a part-time county sheriff's deputy. She was working toward a full-time road patrol position that required her to complete a field training program. Despite her having passed all the requirements and achieved her certifications, she was put on a performance improvement plan, and her employment was subsequently terminated. After the case was settled, the employee was hired by a neighboring county's sheriff's department to perform the same job that she had been denied.

## MEASURING UP

When women and racial minorities complain of disparity in hiring, promotions, and wages, the response is not "That's life!" and laughing it off as irrelevant or amusing. We treat such complaints seriously and give them the importance that they deserve. We expect employers to comply with laws designed to prevent such consequences, and we have provided legal avenues and power to affected employees to pursue lawsuits, if necessary, to enforce these laws. Over the past decade we have begun to treat disparities based on weight and sexual orientation seriously as well, even though weight and sexual orientation are not universally protected by law. But we still treat height prejudice as a trivial matter not worthy of discussion, much less protection. It is as if the rights of short people are more superfluous than everyone else's. There is no good reason why that should be.

Some people contend that height discrimination should not be compared with discrimination based on legally protected categories such as race or gender because it is impossible to regulate all biased behavior. The thinking goes that just because bias exists does not mean that it would be practical to enact laws prohibiting all forms of it. These people argue that Title VII was intended to reverse past systemic discrimination and protect groups who were historically unable to protect themselves through the political process, not to address every possible social bias that may exist in our culture. The people who make these arguments often compare height to other beauty traits such as physical attractiveness, weight, hair color, or eye color. They point to studies that claim that blonds make more than brunettes, overweight people make less than fit people, and men who have hair make more than bald men.[36] And since attractiveness is subjective, and if short people earn less just because they are considered less physically attractive, then that is just the way it is, and having more laws to prohibit it would be a pointless endeavor.

I have not been able to find any actual analysis of these claims regarding hair color or bald people, nor have these studies been presented in a way that would allow their methodologies and conclusions to be reviewed. However, the claim about overweight people making less than fit people is of questionable validity. Upon closer review of the research involving overweight people, the claim does not hold true for all people who are overweight or obese: while heavier white women earned less than thinner white women, there is no difference in wages between overweight and thin black women, and overweight men are paid substantially more than thin men.[37] Thus, the weight wage gap is based more on gender and race than on weight itself. The claim about bald men earning less than hairy men does not even ring true, given that bald men often are perceived as more experienced and authoritative. Perhaps it may be true in certain occupations, but there is no evidence showing that this effect is widespread.

In addition, attractiveness traits like hair color and baldness are purely subjective and can be easily changed or concealed. Overweight people can lose weight. Unlike being overweight or having an undesirable hair color, being short is an inherent trait that cannot be changed or concealed, just like gender or race. Also, while different people may disagree about baldness or a particular hair or eye color as being attractive, being short is a fact that is not subject to interpretation or opinion—one either is or is not short. Because of this, height discrimination is much more like race and gender discrimination than discrimination based on attractiveness or other physical features. And while it would be impossible and unnecessary to address all of our subjective beauty biases with laws, it would not be very difficult to address height discrimination with a few simple tweaks to existing laws.

More importantly, comparing the histories of other prejudices is not really relevant or necessary. No laws are ever enacted with the intention that they must remain unchanged and frozen in their original language in perpetuity. All laws change over time to address current circumstances, either through amendment or through judicial interpretation. Extending the protections of Title VII to obese, short, or LGBT individuals would help spur social change by correcting wrongs that currently exist in our society and would send the message to employers that discrimination is wrong no matter who the target is. In any case, there is no legal or moral justification for the requirement that prejudices must be equivalent or similar to receive legal protection. None of the current categories protected by Title VII are similar to each other.

Adding new categories to the list does not take anything away from

SHORTCHANGED

those who are already covered. If we are going to have antidiscrimination laws at all, then there is no harm in having these laws cover other marginalized groups. It could be argued that by having antidiscrimination laws cover some, but not all, groups of people that need protection, we are in effect favoring some people and singling out others. Those who are not covered receive the message that despite experiencing similar discrimination, they are not worthy of protection. This message further confirms their marginalization and helps to reinforce the social stigma, because there are many people who believe that height discrimination is not wrong because it is not illegal.

Workplace disparities based on height should be treated with comparable dignity and importance as workplace disparities based on legally protected categories, because what is at the root of unequal rights when it comes to race and gender discrimination—disdain and contempt for certain characteristics considered to be inferior—is also at the root of height discrimination. The same kind of disdain and contempt that is manifest in unequal treatment of women and minorities is at play against short people. People prefer that those who are disdained be invisible. They try to ignore them, but if that does not work, they will treat them with increasing disrespect and hostility to attempt to push them back in their place. The end result is that the victim is excluded from opportunities and remains an outsider, unable to break through the glass ceiling to higher level positions and higher pay. Even though most legal challenges based on short stature alone have failed in courts, and some new theories have not been successfully litigated, it is undeniable that height discrimination has serious consequences in the employment context. It does not seem reasonable that harassment and discrimination based on sex, religion, race, national origin, and physical disability are prohibited, while it is acceptable to shame and demean someone, and pay that person les, simply because he or she is short.

It is helpful that Michigan and a handful of municipalities have had the courage to fill the gap in federal law by passing their own antidiscrimination laws. The residents of those jurisdictions are better protected. But addressing this gap in federal antidiscrimination laws is important, because all people deserve to be equal before the law and not be treated differently based on where they happen to reside. If we are going to have federal laws designed to ensure that people are treated according to their individual merits, not by group association, then those laws should cover all marginalized groups. Indeed, the intent behind federal laws is based on the idea that employment decisions and practices that adversely impact certain employees based on an immutable trait are unfair. When these laws were enacted, it was recognized that to have a free and prosperous society, minorities have to be protected. These laws were passed with full knowledge of the existence of social and cultural norms that encourage or tolerate irrational biases. They were designed to protect those individuals who are most likely to be victims of such biases.

Height is an immutable trait, and people who are extremely short are victims of prejudice in our society. Short people are adversely affected by unfair hiring, promotion, and compensation decisions, which should be considered legally impermissible. Like other categories that enjoy a legally protected status, short people share an unusual characteristic that triggers pervasive and irrational prejudice. As a result, they should be considered on an equal footing with other protected groups. If we subscribe to the notion that arbitrary decisions based on height are unfair and immoral, then we should do more to address prejudicial employment decisions, both in our laws and in our workplace policies.

To encourage employers to take height discrimination complaints seriously and enforce compliance, existing laws should be clarified or modified with some simple changes that would help victims of height discrimination overcome obstacles that have proven insurmountable in previous cases. Although some "creative" theories have been proposed to pursue gender stereotyping claims under Title VII, and "normal range" theory may be used under the ADA, such theories have not yet been tried or proven to be successful. Amending Title VII to add height as another category to the list of protected groups or revising its regulations to clarify at what point or under what circumstances height would be considered as protected would send the message to employers that discrimination based on height is as unacceptable as discrimination based on gender, race, religion, or national origin. Extending Title VII protection to cover short people could be critical for the millions of American workers who are employed by state and local government agencies, because plaintiffs are typically barred from bringing ADA suits against government agencies. Nevertheless, it is also warranted to modify or amend the ADA to clarify that height discrimination is prohibited. At the very least, EEOC regulations promulgated under the ADA should be amended or further refined to clarify when exactly short stature falls so far outside of the "normal range" as to constitute an impairment (the measurement of an individual's height percentile in the overall population is an objective standard that cannot easily be disputed).

Absent changes in federal laws and regulations, or even in addition to such changes, state and local governments should follow Michigan's lead to enact laws that extend additional protection against height discrimination, beyond that offered by federal laws. Such legislation should be written clearly to identify the specific height percentiles to which the protection applies, so as to avoid vagueness and provide maximum benefits to the victims of height discrimination. Having access to multiple court systems also would allow victims of height discrimination a variety of remedies and a choice of federal and state courts.

The takeaway for leaders, managers, and HR personnel is that height matters in the employment context just as much as race, gender, or other physical attributes that enjoy legal protection. When considering the absence of racial minorities and women in executive roles, we must also consider that short workers face a similar glass ceiling. In many workplaces, it is often the tallest male who has the leadership role over a group or a team, due to our unconscious deference to physical size. Even in groups led by a woman, she is usually very tall. When considering whether our workplace has a gender or race wage gap, we must also consider whether our workplace has a height wage gap. The lack of representation of short people in leadership positions and highest corporate ranks, and the substantial height wage gap throughout all occupations, demonstrate the existence of bias. The bias may be unconscious, but its effect is significant. It causes people to make irrational choices that are driven by prejudice, choices that make no logical or rational sense, choices that destroy business value. When we discount a job candidate for a job or an employee for a promotion because he or she is black, short, a woman, or whatever, we destroy business value. Even without laws that explicitly prohibit height discrimination, being aware of height discrimination is important for employers because just like discrimination in any other form, it destroys business value. It destroys teams and demoralizes and demotivates employees by undermining their self-confidence, reputation, and ability to perform.

The absence of universal laws prohibiting height discrimination does not signify that the issue does not exist or that it is not important. Passing new laws, or amending existing laws, is not the only way to effect change in society. In the absence of laws, companies may not need to comply with legal mandates that prohibit discrimination, but there is still a valid reason to focus on preventing discrimination, because doing so creates real business value. Social justice issues like discrimination are important not only for society at large but also for business, and business can do as much to advance those goals as new laws. Those companies that have been created in the era of the conscious business movement recognize that commerce has long been a powerful force in shaping society. Conscientious business leaders have an opportunity to be a force for addressing social justice issues in a way that can make as much difference as legislative action. They can play a larger role than individuals when they use their resources to take a stand by donating money or time to social justice organizations. They can also make a big impact when they voice their positions publicly, such as when companies spoke out against laws in Arkansas and Indiana that fostered discrimination against LGBT individuals, and the laws were changed as a result. By supporting social justice ideas and other new perspectives, businesses can be a driving force for social change.

Combating workplace height discrimination is about more than merely alleviating wrongs against individuals. It is also about recognizing the value of diversity in the organization. A truly diverse organization is a better organization. Diversity is about much more than race, religion, and gender. The goal of diversity is to encourage seeking out and developing the best talent and creating an inclusive work environment that values differences—in physical traits as well as thinking styles, education, and socioeconomic status, among other variables. The laws of economics and many studies of diversity have confirmed that if we use the entirety of human talent, our organizational performance will improve. When more people are given opportunities to compete, the overall level of performance naturally increases. Companies will achieve better results (i.e., profits) not only through providing more and innovative products, but also by providing an environment in which all employees can realize their fullest potential. Having an environment like that requires a complete rejection of all forms of discrimination.

In order to build and maintain a diverse and inclusive workplace and a culture that rejects all form of discrimination, executives must take the lead to remove arbitrary barriers such as discrimination and social prejudice. We must redefine discrimination and work to end it in all its forms, including heightism. Short people face many size-related obstacles in the professional world that prevent them from reaching the leadership ranks. When short people act boldly and work to become more powerful, they are deemed to have violated the stereotypical expectation that they should be quiet and obedient, like children. This bias is why short people are held back from the top of the corporate ranks.

If being short is as much of a handicap as race or gender when it comes to success in the workplace, then executives and HR professionals should take steps to address the issue with the same commitment that they use to address other forms of workplace discrimination. Our strategy to build a diverse workforce that values all employees must address not only legally protected classes such as race and gender, but all physical traits, including height and weight, among others. At the core of the issue is the expectation of treating all people with dignity and respect, so it is not important which particular group is experiencing discrimination. All discrimination is wrong.

Organizational leadership creates the culture of its organization. If diversity is an important value to executives, it will be taken seriously by the rest of the organization. If the executives of the organization have an expectation that all of their leaders and managers will maintain an environment that supports all employees, then that culture will prevail. It is up to the executive leadership to establish the right culture, one of inclusion and generosity toward others, in which every employee not only feels respected but in turn is expected to recognize his and her own biases and to act to neutralize them.

To begin with, it is important to raise awareness about the existence of human bias, including height bias, in all people. The best approach is to use scientific data to demonstrate the bias and its effects on the workplace success of various groups of employees. Focusing on scientific data is more effective than simply accusing people of being sexist, racist, heightist, and homophobic, because data show that all of us are human and subject to these biases. By training the entire workforce to be aware of and to understand that bias is part of human nature, they will be predisposed to recognize it in themselves and try to fix it. Awareness of our own bias goes a long way to help us mitigate it in ourselves.

Bias awareness training should cover not just awareness, but also how to apply specific skills to prevent our biases from affecting our behavior. Furthermore, it is important for a workplace diversity effort that people learn not just how to deal with their own biases, but also how to identify potentially biased behavior in others, particularly managers. Everyone in the organization needs to be able to notice bad behavior and feel comfortable speaking up. To this end, it is important that an anonymous hotline be established so that employees can report issues and concerns without fear of reprisal.

In addition, any workplace training related to bias should be coupled with performance management training for managers that provides valuable guidance on how to objectively link performance with business goals while managing their unconscious biases. Perhaps managers automatically associate leadership ability with height, but that does not make that bias rational or in the best interests of the organization. It may be that managers are uncomfortable with people who are not within the "normal" range of heights. But unless the job legitimately requires specific physical size, this comfort level should be challenged as irrelevant. Instead, managers should be required to establish objective performance-based measurements that they will apply when evaluating their direct reports.

Creating an organizational culture that truly values diversity and is inclusive takes a long time and requires discipline and accountability that goes well beyond a single training course in bias awareness. Besides training, each organization should develop workplace policies that promote equity in hiring, compensation, and promotion without regard to inconsequential characteristics such as height. The policies should be backed up by appropriate processes designed to ensure that the lessons learned in training are implemented effectively. Leadership and HR representatives should always be asking themselves: Is a particular manager disproportionately promoting certain employees over others? Are direct reports being assessed objectively? Are reprimands being applied fairly and impartially? There should be an appropriate level of oversight of management decisions involving all aspects of employment: screening job candidates, interviews, the assignment process, mentoring programs, performance evaluations, identifying high performers, promotions, and terminations. Departing employees are an often overlooked trove of useful information about the organization. Conducting exit interviews with former employees at the time of separation is an invaluable tool in understanding what issues they may have faced and whether they would consider coming back.

Efforts to create an unbiased organizational culture must address both the negative and the positive; they must seek not only to eliminate the negative aspects of our biases but also to embrace the positive aspects of an environment that supports all employees. These are two sides of the same coin. An effort to establish and enforce antidiscrimination policies should be coupled with an equal effort to develop a culture in which all employees, regardless of height, gender, race, age, or other characteristic, are treated with respect and encouraged to reach for success, including leadership roles, if that is what they desire.

However, organizational actions alone are not enough; for all employees to feel respected and valued, each individual manager must be responsible for overcoming his or her own natural bias. Critical thinking is the best antidote to bias. After becoming aware of the bias, managers must take the time to understand how it can affect their decisions in ways that may lead to workplace discrimination and make deliberate changes in their behavior that are intentionally designed to lead to more rational decision making. Among the notions that managers and leaders should consider is why short people, women, and minorities tend to lack confidence and tend not to promote themselves, and why when they do act confidently and try to promote themselves, managers have a negative response. When this response is triggered, managers and leaders should step back and take a moment to reflect and evaluate whether and how the response may be motivated by bias. Rather than acting on instinct, a more thoughtful and reasoned approach can lead the manager to respond differently.

In addition to learning to act with reasoned intention rather than based on intuition, managers and leaders have a duty to address thoughtless and insensitive remarks made by others in their presence. Although workplace jokes are beneficial when used to help create a sense of camaraderie, certain jokes must be banned if they can be deemed offensive. To have an inclusive workplace, we must learn to be sensitive to others' differences and not assume that they will appreciate the joke. A manager who hears or reads an inappropriate joke or comment should not ignore it, but should respond quickly and in a manner that suggests that disrespectful behavior will not be tolerated and will not be accepted by the organizational culture. A simple rebuke like "we do not insult people for their physical attributes here" can effectively prevent any future teasing without escalating a small issue into a bigger one. But if a slap on the wrist fails to work, a manager should be prepared to take further action to protect the organization from being degraded by those who may not be a good cultural fit.

Finally, leaders and managers can take actions designed to help short people, along with women and members of minority groups, feel more valued. To be an effective leader, it is important to realize that certain people who have a history of being marginalized tend to be very sensitive about being excluded. To help such employees, a good leader will make a conscientious effort to avoid behaviors that might lead his or her team members to feel discounted or ignored. Truly paying attention to others and reflecting on the issue of bias and discrimination will help to build understanding. An intentional effort to include others is critical to fostering cooperation among team members. To build this sense of inclusion, leaders should practice being more diligent about regularly including all team members in important discussions, allowing them opportunities to explore potential new skills and capabilities, inviting them to a prominent seat at the table, asking for their opinions, and really listening without interrupting or belittling them. In other words, they must mentor them.

When diversity is truly valued in a workplace, and it is not something that just receives lip service, individuals and teams can work together more effectively toward shared goals that benefit not only the organization, but also each of its employees, its customers, and the greater culture. By valuing diversity, employers ultimately empower individuals and the communities in which they live. By supporting equal pay for all their workers regardless of race, gender, height, weight, age, sexual orientation, or any other arbitrary characteristic that has nothing to do with an individual's work performance, employers empower their workers so that they feel more financially secure, which in turn enriches their communities. People who may not have been aware of their biases become inspired to change their attitudes and behaviors, not just at work but also in other aspects of their lives. This greater cooperation among people trickles down beyond work relationships, creating long-term value for society overall.

# FOUR

# a little perspective

IT IS WORTH NOTING that being short does not automatically mean having to lead a second-rate life. In fact, most short people can and do have exciting careers, successful romantic relationships, and happy families. As I hope this book makes clear, height is just a number, and an arbitrary one at that. It has zero effect on a person's personality or character.

While it is good and right to explore the effects of height discrimination, short people should try to keep it in perspective and not let it ruin their lives. Being short is not the end of the world, and most of the hardships we face are unpleasant but manageable. Social stigma does hurt, and we can and should strive to improve the situation, but we can do so without getting ourselves bogged down in a victim mentality. The trick is keeping a sense of perspective and managing ourselves in a way that preserves our emotional health and saves us from unhappiness.

In fact, being short is not all bad. In many respects, it is actually an advantage.

## SLIGHT EVOLUTIONARY EDGE

During the past century the populations of the United States and other prosperous countries have been getting taller. As a result of this shift in the height curve, many scientists have come to associate height with better living standards. Because of this newly acquired scientific significance as a measure of health and well-being, height has been used by scientists and historians as an indicator of health.[1] Some have attempted to use evolutionary advantage arguments to explain our social height bias. The argument contends that tallness is a desirable trait for the purpose of survival of our species, so a taller man will be a better provider (because he earns more money) and will be better able to protect his mate and family (because of his physical strength). Having been chosen through the process of natural selection, the trait continues to be passed down through generations.

Of course this hypothesis does not account for the fact that there are some poor and developing countries, particularly in Africa, where people are quite tall, while some developed first-world nations have relatively short populations. It also ignores the fact that there are many qualities about a person that are desirable besides height. And of course short men and women do usually find mates and procreate just as often as taller people. In other words, the argument that taller height is a result of evolutionary processes is unfounded.

While there are certain physical disadvantages for people who are short; such as having difficulty finding clothes and shoes that fit well; being unable to reach items on higher shelves; and having to use cars, furniture, and large household appliances that may be uncomfortable for shorter bodies, these disadvantages are the result of societal and cultural preferences, rather than biological or natural selection. These supposed disadvantages have no effect on the genetic or evolutionary success of height as a physical trait.

In fact, nature does not share our societal preference for tallness. Nature actually shows a preference for shortness. Increased body height and weight have a harmful impact on the planet by requiring increased energy, resources, water, and food. Shorter people generally eat and drink less than taller people, use less energy, and even use less fabric and other resources.[2] Scientifically, smaller bodies also have an evolutionary advantage over taller bodies. Shorter bodies are more efficient and have a better chance of surviving the stresses of malnutrition and disease. In times of famine, shorter people are more likely to survive.

In addition, being short offers significant advantages when it comes to health. There is a higher incidence of various types of cancer among taller people.[3] Researchers reviewing the Million Women Study in the United Kingdom found that a woman's risk of developing a range of different cancers increased by 13 percent for every ten centimeters of height. Similar conclusions were reached in the Women's Health Initiative study of more than twenty thousand women, based in the United States,[4] in which taller women showed a 13–17 percent greater risk of developing melanoma, breast cancer, ovarian cancer, endometrial cancer, and colon cancer and a 23–29 percent greater risk of developing kidney, rectum, thyroid, and blood cancers. Similarly, taller men have a greater risk of developing certain prostate cancers. Scientists believe that the reason for this is that the cells in a bigger human body require a larger number of duplications, and as organs decline with advanced age, difficulties in replacing defective or dead cells may lead to greater incidence of cancer. Also, shorter people have been shown to have lower rates of cardiac death than taller individuals, based on the fact that they have fewer diet-related chronic diseases, especially after middle age.[5] This may be due to the fact that greater height in childhood promotes adult obesity, and tall children are five times more likely to become obese as adults than shorter children.[6]

Furthermore, more than twenty studies have shown that short people tend to live longer than tall people, by an average of six months for each centimeter of height.[7] The shorter the person, the longer he or she is likely to live. This is further supported by the fact that men are about 9 percent taller than women in almost all human cultures, and women's average life expectancy is approximately 9 percent greater than men's life expectancy in these same cultures.[8] Short men, who are the same height as women, tend to live longer as well. Consider that the residents of Japan's Okinawa islands, where the average male is four foot nine, are also the longest-lived people in the world, have nearly seven times the number of individuals over one hundred years old, and have the lowest rates of cancer and heart diseases of any country in the world.[9]

## SHORT IS POWERFUL

Shorter bodies also have some significant physical advantages over tall bodies. In certain sports in which balance and proportional strength are important, like gymnastics and ice skating, the shorter athletes have a vast advantage over their taller counterparts. This advantage results from the shorter body's lower center of gravity (which provides more balance) and a higher strength-to-mass ratio (which increases their ability to perform moves that require twisting or whole-body rotation). The smaller the body, the more easily it can be propelled through the air. The most elite gymnasts considered to be the best in the world have been extremely short and have continued to get shorter over time: Nadia Comaneci (1976 Olympic all-around champion) is four foot ten, Mary Lou Retton (1984 champion) is four foot nine, and most recently, Simone Biles (2016 champion) is four foot eight. Just as Michael Phelps is "built to be a swimmer" due to his disproportionately long limbs and torso, Simone Biles is "built to be a gymnast" due to her short stature.

Being shorter also makes it easier to succeed in strength sports like bodybuilding and weightlifting, because longer limbs must do more work to achieve the same effect as shorter limbs. It takes more effort to build up a longer muscle than a shorter muscle to a comparable girth, and it takes more effort to lift a barbell to a taller height. Short weightlifters often out-lift taller ones because the athlete with longer arms must cause the barbell to travel a much longer distance. That is why strength sports are dominated by shorter, stocky athletes, while sports that require more dynamic activities, such as sprinting and jumping, are dominated by taller athletes.

Other sports in which short stature can be an advantage include horse racing and car racing (in which being smaller and lighter allows for greater speed) and distance running and distance cycling (in which greater strength relative to length allows for greater endurance). With respect to team sports like soccer, being short may not be a significant advantage but is not a major disadvantage, either; some of the world's best soccer players have been very short, including Andres Iniesta of Spain at five foot seven and Argentina's Diego Maradona at five foot five. Lionel Messi, one of the best soccer players in the world, is reported to be five foot seven, but according to a June 5, 2014, article in the *New York Times Magazine,* that is an exaggeration.[10] Certain positions in soccer, such as midfielder and forward, offer an advantage for shorter players because it is easier for a shorter body to control its limbs and change directions faster. The ability to pivot faster makes it easier for these players to evade the defenders and to squeeze through between taller players. While height may be a distinct advantage for defenders and goalkeepers, being short can be better for offensive positions.

## SOME UPLIFTING WORDS

This book has illustrated some negatives about being short. Yes, short people are often disrespected in the workplace. They get a bad rap in the media. It can be difficult for them to find a date. After facing difficulties and prejudice all their lives, short people sometimes begin to submit to the expectations that we have for them by becoming either timid and insecure or bitter and resentful, which only serves to reinforce those social stereotypes.

But the existence of prejudice does not mean that short people should spend their lives being depressed or angry. Yes, heightism is prevalent in our society, but that does not mean that short people should resign themselves to leading mediocre or unsatisfactory lives. In fact, most short people eventually become well-adjusted because they have learned to deal with and overcome the obstacles related to their stature. As adults, most have good jobs, get married, and have families. There are many amazing, brilliant, and talented short people who have made grand achievements in each and every field and profession, including business, education, sports, arts, and science. Being short may have some disadvantages, but these are challenges that can be overcome while we work toward social change.

When we feel like victims and look for sympathy from others, we are approaching it from a sense of weakness. The victim mentality acknowledges a lack of control. Instead, we must take full responsibility for our own empowerment. When we take the responsibility to build up our own power and self-confidence, we are better able to handle adversity. Our experiences in life, and whether we feel that life is successful and happy or futile and depressing, are determined to a large extent by our own attitudes. When faced with an obstacle, we must own it to the extent we have control, and we have control over our own attitudes and behavior.

It may seem plausible initially that a smaller person should feel less powerful than a larger one, just because of size alone. However, feeling powerful is not related to one's size. A sense of power has more to do with one's mental attitude than actual physical size. In fact, in any relationship the person who feels more powerful is the person who has more leverage. And leverage has less to do with size than with having alternatives.

For instance, consider a negotiation for the sale of a car. The salesperson may be huge and the customer may be small, but it is the customer who has all the leverage in that situation. The customer's physical size is completely irrelevant to his or her negotiating power. The reason for this is that the customer has the option to buy or not buy the car. A customer who thinks, "If this car negotiation doesn't work out, I'll go to the dealership across the street and buy a car there" is indifferent about being able to close the deal. It is that option that gives the customer power in that deal. In fact, the more options the customer has, the more power the customer has in the negotiation. Having other alternatives allows the customer to feel indifferent because he or she can simply walk away if the deal does not work out. That is where power lies.

If having options is what gives us power, then when we find ourselves feeling powerless, we can reduce that feeling by taking specific actions to create more options for ourselves. Consider how powerless a business owner would feel if his business only had one customer. His sense of powerlessness arises from knowing that he would go out of business if he lost that one customer. No business can survive for long with only one customer, because the business is at the mercy of that customer's whims. That business owner should immediately go about marketing his services to attract more customers. Developing multiple customers means having alternatives that allow the business to survive in case any one customer is lost.

The same thought process applies on an individual level. If we feel powerless at work, for example, we can take steps to feel more powerful by creating additional sources of income. Just as a business with only one customer is vulnerable to that customer's whims, when we work for an employer, we are always subject to that employer's whims. The employer can decide at any time to lay us off or terminate our employment, which would leave us without an income. That possibility can leave any employee feeling powerless. To address that feeling, we can take steps to develop multiple streams of income. When our income is not dependent on one source, we can feel less powerless at work, because our other alternatives lessen our fear of losing our jobs. Any time we feel powerless and have the need to develop and expand our options, we should consider the following questions:

What could I do differently?

Whom can I ask for assistance?

Where else can I look for a solution?

What are my criteria for success?

What are some other perspectives that I have not considered?

How can I develop additional skills or knowledge to address this obstacle?

Who has successfully overcome this obstacle, and what can I learn from this person?

Another way to reduce our sense of powerlessness is to develop more confidence. We are unlikely to overcome an obstacle if we do not believe that we are capable of surmounting it. Self-confidence has a lot to do with both how we are perceived by others and how we perceive ourselves. Confidence is an important focus area not just for short people who have low self-esteem, but also for other marginalized groups and those who have been regarded by society as inferior or subordinate. People who have low self-esteem tend to lack professional ambition and self-confidence because they have internalized the message that they should not behave in a way that would be interpreted as too aggressive. They have learned that they should not speak unless spoken to and should behave as we expect children to behave. As these messages are reinforced over a lifetime, they become internalized as an integral part of one's disposition. There is pressure to remain in lower level roles and not even aspire to leadership positions.

Confidence is a quality that cannot be given to someone; it must be developed by each individual. It is vital to work on eliminating those internal barriers that we can control. Only we can control our own thoughts and actions.

Following are some suggestions on how to develop self-confidence. I am not saying that by taking this advice to heart you will never experience height discrimination. After all, it is not the victim of prejudice who causes the prejudice; the victim is not the perpetrator. Your being confident will not prevent another person's bigotry. However, taking this advice has helped many short people learn to cope with and overcome some of the effects of bigotry, and it is a constructive alternative to feeling like a victim.

*1. Physical stature.* Bearing, fitness, and personal grooming all help make the best first impressions. They show the esteem in which we hold ourselves. Accentuating those physical attributes that are not based on height and having a strong body with good posture will go a long way to make a short person appear more confident.

Making a few physical adjustments in posture also can help give the illusion of tallness. Practicing this high-power pose will help lead to a change in mental attitude: realign the body to assume a more dominant pose by sitting up erect, pulling back the shoulders, and spreading the limbs so that they take up as much room as comfortably possible. Another version of this high-power pose is similar to the Superman or Wonder Woman pose: stand with feet shoulder-width apart and hands on the hips, chin up.

Greater confidence in our physical abilities also transforms into more confidence generally. Physical fitness not only builds muscle strength and tone but also provides an important mental edge. Weight lifting and training in the martial arts (which were designed by and have many practitioners who are short) can even be a deterrent against a physical altercation. Learning self-defense techniques not only helps one be prepared for physical attacks, but also helps one feel more confident generally.

The ultimate goal of developing physical fitness is about becoming empowered mentally to take on bullies should the need ever arise. A bully looking for a potential target will most likely go away if the target appears to be ready and willing (and has the real ability) to fight. But most important, immersion in a sport is a good hobby and will provide a fitter body, improved self-esteem, and social interaction with others who have similar interests.

*2. Mental attitude.* Discrimination perpetuated by others is not nearly as destructive as the discrimination we practice against ourselves, through negative internal messages about our own competence, worth, and attractiveness. Developing and displaying a healthy attitude is key. It is not possible to become taller, so the only thing we can control is our own response to being short. Our size is our size; that is the hand we have been dealt, so there is no point in dwelling on it. We do not have to start loving our size, but we should strive to accept it. Wishing to be taller is a waste of time. Accepting our size does not mean we have to love every aspect of our bodies, and it does not mean we should not do everything we can to fight heightism. We may prefer to have been born taller, more beautiful, or with some more favorable personality traits. It is not unhealthy to recognize that we are not perfect. But the fact that we are short does not mean that we should crawl into a hole for the rest of our lives.

Being a victim is a complete waste of time and energy. We should avoid becoming preoccupied with height. It is not the all-encompassing reason for all the bad things that have happened to us. We should not blame short stature for every negative interaction with another person. Most of the time, for most of our lives, other characteristics and circumstances are far more important than our height. Even when an interaction with another person is about our height, it is important to maintain control over our emotions. We choose how we respond to something rude or cruel from another person; we can either be slightly upset or distraught. The intensity of our reaction is a choice we make. We should not allow other people to have so much power over us that their rudeness or hostility can make us feel devastated. If we maintain an aura of indifference these other people, their hostility will not carry as much weight.

Height will no longer be such a major factor when we are busy developing an interesting and friendly personality. Rather than focusing on the drawbacks of being short, we should focus on the benefits. We should recognize that we have had to work twice as hard to prove ourselves in order to be judged as equal and be accepted as serious contenders. Each success or achievement is an incredible triumph, having required greater effort, talent, and ability than it might have taken a taller person. Short people have had to prove themselves to a greater extent than tall people, and so they should take pride in their accomplishments and take credit for their skills and positive character qualities.

Consciously doing things that boost feelings of satisfaction and happiness will support a positive attitude. That means choosing to spend time with people who primarily make us feel better about ourselves and reading books, watching television shows, going to movies, and listening to music that make us feel good. It means avoiding things and people that make us feel sad and angry. How and with whom we spend our time is our decision to make.

3. *Interpersonal relationships.* Ignoring or denying our size does not work; we can try to ignore our height, but other people clearly do not. Even if they have not made an unacceptable comment (yet), they are consciously or subconsciously assessing our skills and intellect based on our size. Sitting silently may be perceived as quiet strength in a tall person but as incompetence and weakness in a short person. It makes us appear timid and leads to our being overlooked completely. Allowing social stereotypes, juvenile jokes, and comments to affect our self-esteem gives away our power to someone else. It is far better to approach such situations with self-assurance.

When first meeting new people, showing self-respect about our own height is a good way to show them that shortness is a topic on which they do not need to dwell. A quick joke can be disarming, as long as it is not too self-deprecating. It lets people know that we are aware that we are short and there is no need for them to point out the obvious. Also, it makes it clear that being vertically challenged is not a big deal to us, so they should not be bothered by it either. Once that is pointed out, everyone can get over the initial awkwardness and get on with establishing the type of relationship we prefer. Make just one small but witty comment, and then move on.

Overdoing humor can be problematic because treating height as a humorous subject actually helps perpetuate the stereotype and reflects the fact of the height bias itself. Acting too much like a jester will make a short person appear anxious or obsessed about shortness. In addition, when facing a bully or someone who is abusing his or her power, using humor is not very satisfying because it avoids confrontation, so the bully never learns how we really feel. It can be tough to display the courage to take a stand against a bully, especially if that bully is a teacher or boss. After a lifetime of receiving the message that we are lowly and weak, it is difficult to be brave. But running away and hiding only leads to depression or worse. It may be intuitive to believe that no one will hurt us if we lay low and keep invisible, if we do not call attention to ourselves, but that is a bad strategy. Usually, the bully will interpret it as weakness.

Ultimately, standing up to the bully is the most effective way to make the abuse stop. Most bullies will give up if we make them see that it does not have the effect they desire. It can be scary to stand up to a bully, but having courage does not mean that we are not afraid; it means that we can act despite being afraid. Developing the right attitude will help us muster the courage to stand up and speak out. At the core of this courage is the self-belief that we are worth defending. This does not mean that we have to actually punch or kick someone; it is about giving people the perception that we will not tolerate any abuse. It is a show of confidence and control. When we feel ready to defend ourselves, we reclaim our power and our entire bearing changes. As a result, other people will perceive that we are not someone that they need to antagonize.

My ten-year-old son was able use the power of self-belief to stand up to a bully. He had been having trouble making friends at his new school after we moved to a new neighborhood. He was becoming withdrawn and quiet, which was very unlike him. One day my son came home upset because a few other boys in his class had been calling him shorty and midget and had refused to play with him during recess. His dad told him, "Next time, look right into their eyes and say in a strong voice 'shut your mouth or I'll shut it for you!'" We made him practice saying that phrase a few times until he could say it with conviction and force. We told him that if they did not stop taunting him, or if someone pushed him, not to be afraid of hitting back. We wanted him to feel he had our permission to do it if he needed to defend himself. We assured him that even if he got in trouble at school for it, we would always support him if he did it in self-defense.

The next day he came home and said that using the phrase had worked. There was never a need to get physical. The other boys backed off and later even invited him to play with them. He has been friends with those boys ever since.

*4. Professional ambition.* Confidence means pursuing professional goals with boldness and energy, in spite of any discouragement from others. It means refusing to stay on the sidelines, maintaining our dignity and not allowing ourselves to be excluded. When faced with rejection, rather than losing confidence, it is important to try again as soon as reasonably possible. Review the failures, attempt to make corrections or adjustments, and then continue to try. Never give up.

Consider Tyrone "Muggsy" Bogues, a five-foot-three athlete who had a fourteen-season career in the National Basketball Association and who was one of the NBA's all-time leaders in assists. Earl Boykins, at five foot five, and Spudd Webb, at five foot seven, are two other very short men who excelled in basketball, a sport we assume requires extraordinary height. In fact, twenty-four players in NBA history have been shorter than five foot nine. So, while short stature has not been common in basketball, it has not been a disqualifying factor. And if short people can successfully play professionally in the NBA, then height should not be a limiting factor in any other job or profession.

Displaying confidence in the workplace requires having the self-assurance to speak out with conviction. It may be a difficult adjustment on both intellectual and emotional levels, but it is something that is solely within our control. By believing in our capabilities, we will eventually eliminate self-doubt and insecurities. Projecting power and confidence will soon lead to feeling powerful and confident. Of course we should never seek to dominate others through force. However, there is a lot of middle ground between dominating others and retreating into a corner. The key is acting assertively but not aggressively. Proper assertive behavior requires using skills of persuasion to state opinions in a respectful manner, rather than attacking or forcing your opinions on others.

It is vital to be aware that acting confidently may raise issues for some people, especially in the workplace. Women, short people, and minorities are often penalized when they act with confidence. The same behaviors that are rewarded in tall white men are viewed as unlikeable in others. While it is easy to advise those who lack confidence to simply speak up more and follow the above guidelines, when they do, they are often interrupted and their ideas are shut down before they even finish speaking. If they persist, they are judged as too aggressive.

Rather than being rewarded for being confident, short people, women, and racial and ethnic minorities who appear too ambitious are often silenced and penalized. They are admonished that their confidence is off-putting and they should act more humbly. They are encouraged to develop confidence, but without appearing disagreeable or obnoxious. It is a double-edged sword, to be sure. But despite that fact, acting with confidence is still a far better alternative than being timid.

People who lack confidence no doubt do many things that hold themselves back, but confidence alone will not change the way people who lack self-confidence are perceived in the workplace, because it is the systemic bias that causes and perpetuates their lack of confidence. Businesses and social institutions retain equal responsibility for promoting and maintaining the biases and prejudices that maintain the status quo. Telling people that they would be promoted to leadership roles if only they were more self-assured is analogous to telling women that they would never be raped if they would just stop dressing provocatively. We must stop blaming the victims for everything that holds them back. We should realize that our social and cultural biases need to be corrected so that people can be free to achieve success. The victims of bias cannot singlehandedly fix the problem simply by becoming more confident. An external problem cannot be corrected by internal effort alone.

Despite these limitations, it has been shown by many studies that acting confidently helps most of the time. While it may not work 100 percent of the time, for the most part people respond positively to confident people regardless of height, race, ethnicity, or gender. Because we generally confuse confidence with ability, many people do not do the mental heavy lifting of looking at a person's ideas and accomplishments before deciding his or her worth. As a result, confident people tend to achieve higher status and are viewed as more capable.

Short people can be just as effective leaders as taller people. While there is a presumption that a short person is weak and incompetent, and a taller leader garners more authority and respect, that is all this is—a presumption. It is not a fact. It is not a truth. It is a presumption based on a stereotype about an irrelevant physical characteristic. A person is no more or less likely to be an effective leader whether that person is tall or short, thin or fat, blue-eyed or brown-eyed, blond or red-haired. While our height bias has led to many short people being overlooked for leadership roles, what really matters in leadership is how the person acts, not how he or she looks.

Knowing that the height bias exists, however, short people should keep that fact in mind and make a conscious decision to consistently cultivate calmness and act with dignity in a way that will encourage others to show them respect. When our minds are calm, we naturally can be more creative and effective than when we are emotional. For example, those in a leadership role are more likely to gain respect from others if they demonstrate expertise in their field, humility about themselves, and consideration toward others. Exceptional leaders often take the time to really listen to and understand other people and have gained emotional maturity and self-control so that when confronted by hostility or aggression, they are able to refrain from reacting with anger or other emotions. They act with dignity at all times.

While these qualities are important for every leader, they are particularly important for short men and women in leadership roles, because though a tall leader may be forgiven for occasionally letting down his guard, a short leader can never get away with it. Many tall leaders have been allowed to ascend the corporate ladder without having to prove their competence. Short leaders must always be prepared to demonstrate their expertise.

In addition, given human nature, short people in leadership roles may be tested from time to time by those who cannot resist an underhanded put-down. It is important to be prepared for such an occurrence and not let it catch you off guard. Short leaders should strive to never allow anyone to see their emotions get the better of them, because even one emotional response to a show of disrespect can become fodder for future criticism and insults.

Instead, a more dignified response is one that shows maturity and control. Pausing for a second or two allows you to show wisdom and lets you calm down in the privacy of your own mind. Two effective communication tools used by highly respected leaders are paraphrasing and redirection.

Paraphrasing is a device to show that you are actively listening to another person in a way that will make him or her more willing to listen to you. Instead of reacting immediately, take the time to rephrase or sum up what the other person has said: "If I heard you correctly, you said. . . ." By doing this, you demonstrate that you were actively listening to and really heard and understood the person. It also provides an opportunity for the other person to make a correction. Paraphrasing is not the same thing as conceding or agreeing with what was said; rather, it is best seen as a technique that can be used to clear up a miscommunication.

When the other person's focus is on something inappropriate, such as the topic of height, the best thing to do is to redirect attention away from it and toward a more appropriate topic. Redirection is taking the opportunity to change the conversation toward what you want it to be.

Following is an example involving a "harmless" joke:

OTHER: Sorry, I didn't even see you down there. You should stand up! Oh, you're already standing.

YOU: [*Pause for one or two seconds.*] Hmmm. If I heard you correctly, you said that I'm too small to be visible. We do not insult people here for their physical attributes. Let's go ahead and start the meeting by discussing the status of Project XYZ.

In the next example, you have rejected a request and the other person interprets your decision as reflecting your character rather than being based on the merits:

OTHER: All you short people sure have a complex.

YOU: [*Pause for one or two seconds.*] I understand that you're concerned that my rejection of your proposal has something to do with my character or mental health rather than the merits of your request. In fact, I rejected your request because of [*specify reasons X, Y, and Z*]. Now let's move on to discussing. . . .

# *altimate change*

Height says nothing
about the character
of an individual,
but it says a great deal
about the character
and values of a society.
STEPHEN S. HALL

## SUMMING IT ALL UP

In our culture, short people suffer discrimination in ways that are some-times blatant and sometimes subtle. Children who are short but other-wise healthy and normal are treated too often as though they have some sort of disease requiring medical intervention. Short employees experi-ence workplace discrimination when it comes to hiring, promotion, and earning equal pay that is on a par with the discrimination experienced by women and racial and ethnic minorities, but they do not enjoy the same legal protections as women and minorities. Air bags in cars, which have been designed to be a safety feature, instead pose an incremental risk of injury to short people. Even more "trivial" issues like amusement park rides that prevent short children from joining their taller friends and grocery store shelves that make it difficult for short shoppers to reach a product are symptomatic of how manufacturers do not take into account the needs of short people when designing products. In addition, the widespread negative portrayal of short people in the media and the myriad other minor inconveniences that short people deal with every day compound the problem of the social stigma against short people, because they imply that treating short people with disrespect is normal and disregarding their needs is socially acceptable.

The human inclination to prejudge people because they are short is a natural instinct, but its effects are offensive. As a society that values equality and respect for each individual, we should work collectively to reduce and eliminate heightism with no less diligence than we use when addressing other types of bigotry. If we can have public debate and discourse about prejudice related to race, ethnicity, religion, gender, sexual orientation, and physical disabilities, then we can do likewise about other physical differences such as height. Whether one agrees or disagrees with some or all of the premises asserted in this book, the time has come for us to begin engaging in a public exchange of ideas regarding this topic.

As a society we have come to hold the fundamental value of diversity and of treating all people with equal dignity and respect. We no longer consider it morally or socially acceptable to make fun of someone based on race, class, religion, gender, or disability. People who persist in using politically incorrect slurs are told to shut up; they are rarely given a platform to disseminate such ideas without an accompanying backlash. To reinforce our social values, we have enacted laws to protect people against discrimination on the basis of race, color, religion, gender, age, physical disability, and national origin. Antidiscrimination laws attempt not only to make people in these categories equal in the eyes of the law, but also to encourage a cultural shift toward more respect and equal treatment in social interactions. The laws are intended to address historical wrongs as well as to reeducate the public and enable the moral values of nondiscrimination to trickle down from legal mandate to everyday dealings among people. As the July 7, 2014, BBC news program about John Bercow cited previously concluded, height prejudice is morally acceptable because height discrimination is not protected by law. Therefore to change that kind of misguided attitude, we must change the law.

Since the Civil Rights Act was enacted in 1964, our society has been undergoing a sea change not just in formal government-related or employment matters but also in how protected groups are treated in social relationships. Behaviors previously considered socially acceptable, such as catcalling to a woman walking by on the street or calling a black man "boy," are no longer socially tolerated. The prejudice faced by African Americans in the United States has been the focus of much attention since the 1960s. During the ensuing decades, the attitudes of white people in American society toward African Americans have been in the process of undergoing a shift. After reading about racial issues, studying them in schools and universities, hearing about them in the media, and watching movies and television shows about them, many white Americans' perceptions of African Americans has changed from what they were before the 1960s. The social discourse about this subject has led many people to contemplate their own behavior and to pay more attention during their interactions with African Americans. The shift has not been universal, nor have the society's biases been eliminated, but a big improvement has been made. While certainly insufficient and no doubt too slow in coming, it is undeniable that substantial progress has been made since the civil rights movement began, and it is continuing.

The same has been true of how the social discourse initiated by the feminist movement in the late 1960s and 1970s started a shift in attitudes about women and sexism. There has been substantial, albeit still insufficient, progress in equality between men and women and in the general treatment of women in our society. True equality between the sexes and among different races and creeds has not yet been achieved, but progress has been made because of the extensive dialogue and attention that have been directed to these issues.

Likewise, much has been written about prejudice against different kinds of historically disadvantaged groups such as Hispanics, Native Americans, and Asians in the United States; Jews in Europe; Aborigines in Australia; and people with disabilities. All countries and societies have a group or groups of people that have been victims of prejudice. During the past few decades, new issues like obesity, transgenderism, and sexual orientation have been introduced into the cultural discourse, and we have been inundated with information and calls for being more sensitive and respectful in our dealings with people who fall into one or more of these categories.

Since about the mid-1980s, we have seen a dramatic transformation in laws, politics, and societal attitudes regarding lesbian, gay, bisexual, and transgender individuals. This shift in social attitudes toward bisexual and homosexual individuals is happening despite the fact that nothing about their outward appearance announces anything that may be considered socially undesirable. As more gay and lesbian actors began to come out of the closet and started to be more openly represented in movies and on television, more support groups were formed in schools and colleges and more public discourse took place everywhere in our society, leading to the passage of laws that overruled bans on gay marriage. Over time, homophobic jokes that used to be socially acceptable have come to be considered disrespectful and repulsive and are now rightly challenged in polite society.

The cultural shift toward more inclusiveness is the result of extensive dialogue and debate about our inherent instinct to stereotype, about social prejudice and the tendency to discriminate against those who are different. As a result of all this discourse, many of us have become more aware of our own attitudes. This awareness has prodded us to start noticing how our behavior is perceived and how it affects others. By understanding the effects that stereotyping and biases have on those who are different, we can start to address and try to bring an end to societal intolerance. We do this because it is part of our humanity to work toward the social well-being of our fellow humans, and we cannot accomplish our goals until we help all the individuals in our society feel included. To do so, we must resist the stereotypes associated with a person's physical or ethnic characteristics and resist equating such characteristics with a person's value or character.

While it may be true that racism, sexism, and homophobia are far from extinct, and that even in polite society, bigotry is often just barely under the surface and manifests itself in more subtle ways, we can still say some progress has been made, because it is no longer overt, socially acceptable, legally permitted, in-your-face bigotry. We must accept that bit of progress because we understand that progress is a process along a continuum. At least we are on the right path, persistently pursuing ever-greater acceptance of differences. Our goal is to try to stay on this path and continue to work toward the ultimate destination of full acceptance and equality, even if it may never be completely reached to everyone's satisfaction.

The issue of height discrimination has not even made it to the first stage of the progress continuum. Height discrimination is still overt, socially acceptable, legally permitted, in-your-face bigotry. We have not even made any headway in bringing about awareness of the issue or begun working toward making height differences socially acceptable and legally protected.

## CHECK YOUR TALL PRIVILEGE

Those who do not themselves experience height prejudice or deliberately pay attention to it probably do not notice it. Even if they notice it, they may not consider it important. But instead of dismissing this issue as trivial and unworthy of further discussion, we must take some personal responsibility to build awareness of how heightism affects the short people in our lives and how it is formed by our unconscious biases. We can recognize that we may harbor unintentional bias from time to time, but we can also use our powers of reason and logic to work toward the reduction and elimination of this inadvertent bias. Only through awareness can we learn to mitigate and prevent our biased reactions. Bias is not a human evil; ignorance is.

Those of us who happen to be average height or taller should check their own tall privilege. The belief that tall people should enjoy some sort of social privilege solely by virtue of their height and that they are entitled to their positions of power and authority is both an advantage and a curse. It can be disheartening to consider that all these advantages are instinctively granted for something that is an accident of nature—totally arbitrary and unearned. Being lucky enough to be born with tall genes means that not all the benefits associated with it have been deserved. Some might rightly question whether tall people who earn more money or occupy leadership positions have truly earned them, and whether their talents, abilities, and skills actually contributed to their accomplishments and bigger salaries.

The social deference that is granted to the taller individual sometimes begets the presumption of deferential treatment. Some tall individuals not only experience privilege but eventually come to expect it. While most tall people are often unaware of the advantages they enjoy simply from being tall, some behave as though they are entitled to such advantages. In group settings, it is the tallest individual who tends to take the lead. The fact that tall people's view of the world is shaped by their own vantage point is not their fault, but as a result of this viewpoint, tall people are sometimes blind to how they may overshadow the shorter people around them. Why should this matter to tall people? Because discrimination should matter to everyone. When we know that others suffer from prejudice, or when we ourselves benefit from such discrimination, we have a moral duty to resist its influence. From the point of view of what would most benefit society, selecting leaders who lack the empathy to understand others can lead to poor results for everyone under those leaders' authority.

Tall people can help counteract the negative side effects of this privilege by developing cooperative skills; seeking solutions; using the skills of persuasion, logic, and reason; and adopting a spirit of equality and partnership. By developing the ability to understand and adopt another person's viewpoint, a tall person can become a more empathetic and thoughtful person, as well as a better leader. To understand a short person's point of view, a tall person should intentionally make the effort to consider the short person's goals, qualifications, opinions, life experiences, and internal limitations. The best way to start is to think before speaking, ask questions, and really listen to the answers. It is important to remain aware of giving others' ideas equal weight.

In a social context, it is time for all of us, short and tall, to pay more attention to the daily subtle power plays and humiliations that we inflict on each other and instead focus our efforts on inclusion and mutual respect. There is no need to tease or even point out the obvious by telling short people that they are short or asking how tall they are. Short people also will not consider it funny to hear again that joke about how you almost didn't see them there. Unless you know them very well and are certain that they will not be offended, steer clear of teasing and offensive questions about whether they shop for clothes and shoes in the children's department or are a dwarf or midget. These questions are very disrespectful, especially when addressed to a stranger or mere acquaintance. Furthermore, refrain from behaviors that violate short people's sense of personal space: do not pat them on the head, use them as an arm rest, or attempt to pick them up. Try to be considerate when around short people, including being mindful of where your elbows, handbag, backpack, or other item may be in relation to their heads. Most of all, be cognizant of not defining them by their height or assuming that their personality, character, or mental health are related to their height.

If you find that the short people around you are often angry, it might be because you are treating them disrespectfully, and not because they have a complex. Just as it would be morally repugnant to assume personality traits based on a person's skin color, and just as it would be ridiculous to assume personality traits based on a person's eye color, so it is wrong to assume that short people who are acting angry and hostile or timid and insecure are acting that way because they are short. These are natural human reactions to being insulted. Even if you feel that you are being particularly witty, your comments may be interpreted as patronizing and condescending. You should not be surprised by someone's indignation after you have just tried to dismiss or belittle that person. The worst possible thing to say at that moment is "don't take it personally" or "don't be so sensitive." Instead, it would be best to apologize.

Consider that perhaps it is your contempt that is at the root cause of the issue, not the short person.

Even people who consider themselves to be open-minded and progressive have a tendency to stereotype others based on physical stature without realizing that they are doing anything wrong or disrespectful. Stereotyping is something we humans tend to do instinctively, and despite our best efforts, we continue to harbor some unintentional biases. Indeed, our biases are part of human nature and will persist on some level. But we cannot continue to ignore their impact. There are times when we must act against our inclinations. Our tendency to prejudge may be deeply ingrained, but it is not predestined. We are more intelligent than that. We can make the choice to act either reflexively or reflectively. One of the things that makes humans unique from all other animal species is our cognitive ability to use reason and logic to temper and overcome undesirable instincts that negatively affect our social and cultural success.

Once we have made a moral judgment that reducing and eliminating our bias is the right thing to do, we can choose to act on it. By becoming aware of the tendency to categorize people into inferior and superior groups, of our unintentional biases and their effects on our children, friends, and coworkers, we can begin to become more observant about these differences in both ourselves and others. Based on our observations, we can then begin to control our impulse to prejudge people's character and value on the basis of their physical differences. We can exercise our powers of reason and self-control to restrain our behavior if it is based on irrational or emotional instincts. Our humanity demands that we begin to pay attention to this social ill and work to eliminate it as we work to eliminate other types of prejudice. Our moral judgments about other people should be based on reasons and facts, not on instinct or gut feelings.

As we get older and (hopefully) wiser and more mature, we learn that the most important thing about someone's character is rarely how the person looks. Tall, short, blond, dark, fat or thin—who cares? We realize that what really matters about a person is how considerate, resourceful, smart, and determined he or she is. We learn that initial observations about people are superficial and plastic, rarely representing the whole richness of a person's character. We become more tolerant of others' differences and develop deeper insights about other people. Our higher social values, such as empathy, altruism, cooperation, compassion, and fellowship, must be nurtured to overcome our instinctive biases. It is these types of skills and attributes that will build respect and dignity for all members of our society.

The extent of our development and acceptance of these attributes reflects our own emotional intelligence and maturity. Of course all human beings are biased, and we all have our opinions. We have biases and opinions for a reason. We cannot just throw them aside. But we also cannot allow them to rule who we are. We cannot allow our instinctive biases and opinions to control how we approach situations and people if we know or suspect that our approach will be considered insulting and dehumanizing. If we hold to the value that we should not deliberately do something to offend or harm another person, then after becoming aware that our height bias may be considered offensive, we must recognize our own prejudices and behaviors that are inconsistent with those values.

### MAKING A GRAND DIFFERENCE

Short people are often advised to act more confidently. Well-meaning family and friends often counsel short children that if they will be more self-confident, they will not be mistreated by others. While the recommendation to act confidently is good advice, the idea that confidence is the cure for heightism is misguided. It is important that people begin to understand that it is not lack of confidence that causes inequality; it is our social and cultural biases. While people are responsible for their part in eliminating their own self-doubt and insecurities, our society also has a vital role to play. The problem of low self-confidence must be addressed by the people themselves as well as by society, on both fronts at the same time. It will not go away only by individuals working to address their inner issues because height prejudice is not just personal; it is systemic. The victims of prejudice are not responsible for the prejudice and cannot make changes in themselves that will eliminate another person's prejudice. Yes, we should encourage people to build their own self-confidence, but at the same time we should be focusing on breaking down the social and cultural barriers that stand in their way.

Changing the status quo takes more than just complaining. Social attitudes are not going to change by themselves; we have to make it happen. Real, lasting impact will require working together as a group, both on a national level and locally in every community, school, and workplace. We should put pressure on all aspects of society to demand change.

The first step is building awareness. Disrespect toward short people in the media, in the workplace, and in all different types of interpersonal relationships is nothing more than patent bigotry that should be banished from acceptable behavior. It is time to stop pretending that this issue does not exist. There are millions of short people in this country with their own stories to tell about their experience. We should band together and become activists. We should take our stories to the media and force a dialogue about the issues that concern us.

One of the most depressing facts about heightism is the complete lack of acknowledgment of the issue by short people themselves. It is true that short people display as much bias as tall people against those shorter than themselves. Becoming aware of heightism means becoming aware not only of other people's prejudice but also of our own. It also means becoming aware of our own responses to other people's prejudice. All of us, both tall and short, must acknowledge how cultural stereotypes and biases perpetuate the status quo and strive to rise above them.

To begin raising awareness, we must realize that we are all responsible for confronting heightism when we see it, on all fronts, directly, by speaking out boldly and demanding respect in all aspects of our lives—socially, at school, and at work. We should be vocal in our negative response to any jokes and slurs about short stature, so that they come to be seen by society as unacceptable and as unwelcome as racist and sexist jokes. We should refuse to tolerate name-calling like *midget, manlet, shrimp,* or *little girl/boy,* regardless of whether the offender is tall or short. We should speak out when people make disparaging assumptions about the character or mental health of short people on the basis of height. When we fail to respond, we implicitly approve and condone such teasing. It is everyone's responsibility to speak out forcefully against it.

As more and more of us gather the courage to let the world know there is a problem, this issue will become more widely known, and short people can begin to unify. If we can form a movement, we can more effectively work toward eliminating the ignorance that leads to societal bias against short people. When short people start acting in solidarity in the face of hostility, things can begin to change. In order to get there, short people must stop being so quiet about their own plight and begin to be a driving force for change.

The second step is dialogue. Height bias and discrimination deserve the same attention and public discourse that racism, sexism, and homophobia have received over the past few decades. Height prejudice is pervasive in our culture, but it has never been openly acknowledged or debated. There are no college courses that study height discrimination, and very little scientific research has been done on the topic. We should debate whether it is morally and ethically acceptable that healthy children are labeled as abnormal and subjected to medical bioengineering in an effort to force them into a more socially acceptable ideal. We should debate whether it is acceptable that short employees are judged not by their objective performance and ability but by something as trivial as physical stature when it comes to pay equality and promotions. We should debate whether it is appropriate for our country to have laws against discrimination based on some physical traits but not others. We should question why height should not be considered just as worthy of legal protection as race, gender, religion, ethnicity, and sexual orientation. Whether one agrees or disagrees that these issues are of social significance, the subject is ripe for public discourse.

While some people will be open and receptive to these ideas, initially we can expect a great deal of backlash from those who are just sick and tired of yet another "-ism," those who cannot bear to listen to one more call for political correctness, those who already feel overwhelmed by their social justice obligations. To overcome their objections, it is best to redirect the conversation from political correctness to emotional correctness. Recognize that people who are offended by the idea that short people should expect and demand to be treated with respect are themselves emotionally immature or have not properly thought things through. Keep in mind that after all, it is far more important if a person says or does something disrespectful out of a desire to intentionally and personally hurt another person, as opposed to out of mere ignorance. To persuade those who may not be predisposed to our message, we must first build a foundation for discussion by focusing the conversation on emotional intelligence. We should postpone referring to concepts like discrimination and prejudice and instead focus on the higher order ideals like compassion, empathy, and wisdom. Only then can we begin to build common ground. We will not be able to get people to agree with us if they do not listen to us first.

The third step is action. Once we acknowledge that discrimination exists, we have a duty to resist it where possible. On an individual level, we must make an effort to train our brains to make counterstereotypical associations. For example, rather than watching shows and movies that negatively depict short people in stereotypical roles as clowns or sidekicks, we could watch shows and movies that depict short characters in a dignified way. Also, we can make more of an effort to try to take the perspective of a short person by asking ourselves what our perspective might be if we were in their shoes. Doing so helps raise the level of empathy and reduces biased thoughts about others.

On a societal level, real, meaningful change is about stopping height bias before it turns into discrimination, in schools and in our communities. We need to create an environment for our children that ensures they will not experience bullying from other kids and insensitive comments from adults. It is not enough to just enroll short children in self-defense classes and lecture them about self-confidence. Schools have a responsibility to make all kids feel safe and to feel included and respected for who they are. And it is important for children to learn why people discriminate against physical differences, including height.

School administrators must ensure that existing antibullying materials used by schools include information about short stature among other differences. It is one thing for children to learn bias from their parents, but at least schools can do something to challenge those ideas.

We also should insist on meaningful legal reform. Federal antibullying laws should support victims of bullying regardless of "why" they are being bullied. Federal and state laws should be reviewed and amended to ensure clarity that workplace discrimination on the basis of height will no longer be tolerated, that all workers deserve equal pay and opportunities for advancement at work. Because height discrimination is so unknown, passing such laws will require pressure both politically and socially.

Achieving equality under the law will take a long time, but in the meantime we must work collectively to change cultural and social attitudes by speaking out and organizing a movement. In this task, short people have much to learn from the civil rights, feminist, and LGBT movements. As our country has experienced from the fervor with which these movements pursued their goals, in order to achieve real change and work to eliminate height discrimination in our society, what is needed is a concentrated grassroots effort that will chart a plan that includes bold demands. We must create a detailed agenda that outlines the specific changes needed in employment laws and develop a model for action that covers activities such as protesting and campaigning for change. We must become involved in political campaigns of those politicians who care about equality and urge them to push this agenda. We must create pressure by organizing protests, letter campaigns, and other techniques that have been proven successful for other grassroots movements.

Historically, media and the Internet have not been sympathetic to the plight of short people, but an organized movement can begin to use them as tools to take our message to a broader audience. We should act collectively to challenge insulting portrayals of short people in movies, television shows, and advertisements. We should make a more concerted effort to use media and the Internet to educate the public and to demand a more dignified and respectful portrayal of short people.

Such efforts are not without precedent. From the advent of movies and television, LGBT characters have been portrayed in a disrespectful light. Currently the entertainment industry conducts an annual survey of how LGBT individuals are represented in major Hollywood films. In 2015 the GLAAD Studio Responsibility Index showed that out of 114 studio films, only 20 had LGBT characters of any kind, and most were in tangential roles or represented in an offensive light. The entertainment industry also studies the percentage of characters who are racial and ethnic minorities. There is no reason why it could not begin conducting similar reviews of how short characters are represented in films and television. Armed with information, we can better use social media, Web sites, and blogs to demand more positive portrayals of short people, including demanding new content, news reporting, movies, and television shows about short people's encounters with discrimination and aggression.

The time has come to stop keeping silent and pursue social and cultural change that will lead to more dignity for and respect toward short people. True equality will be achieved only when all people fight against the stereotypes and systemic barriers that hold people back because of race, gender, height, or other inherent traits. Rather than allow current social norms to be perpetuated, we must work to change them and to embrace the virtue of equality. This includes not just the people who fall into one of the legally protected categories, but all those who face discrimination of any kind.

If we want our children, male or female, white or nonwhite, gay or straight, tall or short, to have equal opportunity to pursue and attain whatever goals they set for themselves, then we must work to combat the stereotypes that hold them back. On this, we must all work together. It is time to evolve beyond our instinctual preference for tallness by focusing on our more highly evolved human traits that are associated with emotional intelligence and maturity. Everyone benefits when we display more altruism, empathy, and equality, the values that we learn with wisdom. Courage to act will lead to greater equality and eventually to cultural transformation that will benefit everyone. According to John Stuart Mill, a nineteenth-century philosopher and the first member of the English Parliament to call for women's suffrage, "every great movement must experience three stages: ridicule, discussion, adoption." Let's get started.

# NOTES

## ONE | HEIGHT MATTERS

1. Mazzocco, P., Brock, T., Brock, G., Olson, K., and Banaji, M. "The cost of being black: White Americans' perception and the question of reparations." *Du Bois Review: Social Science Research on Race.* 2006; 3: 261–297.

2. Dubreuil, Benoit. *Human Evolution and the Origins of Hierarchies: The State of Nature.* New York: Cambridge University Press, 2010.

3. Roberts, J. V., and Herman, C. P. "The psychology of height: An empirical review." In C. P. Herman, M. P. Zanna, and E. T. Higgins (Eds.), *Physical Appearance, Stigma, and Social Behavior.* Hillsdale, NJ: Erlbaum, 1985.

4. Bruner, J. S., and Goodman, C. C. "Value and need as organizing factors in perception." *Journal of Abnormal and Social Psychology.* 1947; 42: 33–44.

5. Bruner and Goodman, "Value and need."

6. Stulp, G., et al. "Tall claims? Sense and nonsense about the importance of height of US presidents." *The Leadership Quarterly.* 2012; 24: 159–171.

7. Schubert, Thomas W. "Your highness: Vertical positions as perceptual symbols of power." *Journal of Personality and Social Psychology.* 2005; 89(1): 1–21.

8. Schubert, "Your highness."

9. Stulp, G., et al. "Human height is positively related to interpersonal dominance in dyadic interactions." *PLoS ONE.* 2015; 10(2): e0117860.

10. Maner, J., and Baker, M. "Dominance, evolutionary." In *Encyclopedia of Social Psychology,* 2007; 262–263. SAGE Reference online. http://www.sageereference.com/socialpsychology/Article_n158.html.

11. Stulp et al. "Tall claims?"

12. "Height in inches for females and males aged 20 and over: United States, 2007–2010." Anthropometric Reference Data for Children and Adults: United States, 2007–2010. Vital and Health Statistics, US Department of Health and Human Services, Series 11, Number 252, October 2012.

13. Frankel, Ellen. *Beyond Measure: A Memoir About Short Stature & Inner Growth.* Nashville, TN: Pearlsong Press, 2013.

14. Yancey, G., and Emerson, M. "Does height matter? An examination of height preferences in romantic coupling." *Journal of Family Issues.* 2016; 37(1): 1–21. doi: 10.1177/0192513X13519256.

15. Anderson, R. "The role of height, gender and self-awareness in character perception: Who benefits?" n.d. https://gustavus.edu/psychology/files/Anderson.pdf.

16. Kois, Dan. "Peter Dinklage was smart to say no." *New York Times Magazine.* March 29, 2012.

17. Kois, "Peter Dinklage was smart to say no."

18. "House of Commons speaker John Bercow asks if heightism is acceptable." *BBC News.* July 7, 2014. www.bbc.com/news/uk-28205453.

19. Bump, Philip. "Here's how tall Marco Rubio and everyone else running for president is." *Washington Post.* January 7, 2016; Andrews, Natalie. "Voters size up 2016 presidential candidates: Who's the Tallest?" *Wall Street Journal.* October 27, 2015; Schwab, Nikki, "Who's too short to be president?" *U.S. News.* July 8, 2015; "Graphic: How tall are the 2016 Republican candidates?" *Fox & Friends.* September 17, 2015; Morin, Natalie, "The presidential candidates ranked from smallest to tallest." InsideGov.Com, September 3, 2015.

20. Durkin, J. D. "Is Marco Rubio too short for the presidency? Mediaite examines this 'growing' concern." Mediaite.com, February 24, 2016.

21. Fricker, Martin. "Budding reality TV star Jonathan McNally killed himself 'because he thought he was too short.'" *Mirror.* September 10, 2014.

22. O'Brien, Carl. "They found a note. . . . He was sick of being small, of being teased about his height . . . small things: Typical teenage problems." *Irish Times.* November 1, 2010.

23. Warren, Lydia. "Boy, 13, commits suicide 'after he was bullied for years for being small.'" *Daily Mail.* July 21, 2014.

24. "Did bullying drive 12-year-old East Harlem boy to commit suicide?" *CBS New York.* May 31, 2012.

25. Walden, Tiffany. "Lamar Hawkins suicide: 'Our hearts are broken,' mother says." *Orlando Sentinel.* March 20, 2017.

26. Bult, Laura. "Family says West Virginia boy, 9, was driven to suicide by bullying at school." *New York Daily News.* September 15, 2016.

27. Vargas, B., Canton, J., et al. "Complications of Ilizarov leg lengthening: A comparative study between patients with leg length discrepancy and short stature." *International Orthopaedics.* 2007 Oct; 31(5): 587–591.

28. Moorhead, Alana. "Short people in India endure surgery to have their legs lengthened . . . so they can marry well and get a good job." *The Sun,* May 9, 2016.

29. Moorhead, "Short people in India."

1. Hargreaves, K., Cameron, M., et al. "Is the use of symphysis-fundal height measurement and ultrasound examination effective in detecting small or large fetuses?" *Journal of Obstetrics and Gynaecology* 2011 Jul; 31(5): 380–383.

2. Hall, Stephen S. *Size Matters: How Height Affects the Health, Happiness, and Success of Boys—and the Men They Become.* Boston: Houghton Mifflin Harcourt, 2006.

3. Hall, *Size Matters.*

4. Lipman, T., Hench K., et al. "A multicentre randomised controlled trial of an intervention to improve the accuracy of linear growth measurement." *Archives of Disease in Childhood* 2004; 89: 342–346.

5. Kaplowitz, Paul, and Baron, Jeffrey. *The Short Child: A Parent's Guide to the Causes, Consequences and Treatment of Growth Problems.* New York: Hachette Book Group, 2006.

6. Hall, *Size Matters.*

7. Kaplowitz and Baron, *The Short Child.*

8. Sinha, Sunil. "Short stature." Emedicine. August 1, 2014. http://misc.medscape.com/pi/android/medscapeapp/html/A924411-business.html.

9. Kaplowitz and Baron, *The Short Child.*

10. Kaplowitz and Baron, *The Short Child.*

11. Bucher, D. "Ethical considerations: Growth hormone treatment in children with idiopathic short stature." *Online Journal of Health Ethics.* 2007; 4(1).

12. Kaplowitz and Baron, *The Short Child.*

13. Voss, L. "Is short stature a problem? The psychological view. *Society of the European Journal of Endocrinology.* 2006; 155: S39–S45.

14. Leschek, E., et al. "Effect of growth hormone treatment on adult height in peripubertal children with idiopathic short stature: A randomized, double-blind, placebo-controlled trial." *Journal of Clinical Endocrinology and Metabolism.* 2004; 87(7): 3140–3148.

15. Bucher, "Ethical considerations."

16. Voss, "Is short stature a problem?"

17. "OpportunityAnalyzer: Growth hormone deficiency—Opportunity analysis and forecast to 2024." August 1, 2015. GlobalData report code GDHC029POA.

18. Kaplowitz and Baron, *The Short Child.*

19. Kaplowitz and Baron, *The Short Child.*

20. Tauber, M., Moulin, P., et al. "Growth hormone retesting and auxological data in 131 GHH-deficient patents after completion of treatment." *Journal of Clinical Endocrinology & Metabolism.* 1997; 82(2): 352–356.

21. Kelnar, C., Albertsson-Wikland, K., et al. "Should we treat children with idiopathic short stature?" *Hormone Research.* 1999; 52(3): 150–157.

22. Deodati, A., and Cianfarani, S. "Impact of growth hormone therapy on adult height of children with idiopathic short stature: systematic review." *British Medical Journal.* 2011; 342: c7157.

23. Deodati and Cianfarani, "Impact of growth hormone therapy," c7157.

24. Tarim, O. "Height predictions by Bayley-Pinneau method may misguide pediatric endocrinologists." *Turkish Journal of Pediatrics.* 2013; 55: 485–492.

25. Bucher, "Ethical considerations."

26. Bucher, "Ethical considerations."

27. Poidvin, A., Touzé, E., et al. "Growth hormone treatment for childhood short stature and risk of stroke in early adulthood." *American Academy of Neurology.* 2014; 83: 780–786.

28. Cohen, P. "Serum insulin-like growth factor-I levels and prostate cancer risk—interpreting the evidence." *Journal of the National Cancer Institute.* 1998; 90(12): 876–879; and Hankinson S., Willet W., et al. "Circulating concentrations of insulin-like growth factor I and risk of breast cancer." *Lancet.* 1998; 351(9113): 1393–1396.

29. Rainwater N., Sweet, A. A., Elliott, L., et al. "Systematic desensitization in the treatment of needle phobia for children with diabetes." *Child & Family Behavior Therapy* 1988; 10: 19–31.

30. Sandberg, D., Burkowski, W., et al. "Height and social adjustment: Are extremes a cause for concern and action?" *Pediatrics.* 2004; 114(3): 744–750.

31. Watson, A. "Safety of growth hormone." *Lancet.* 1991; 337: 108.

32. Walker, J., Bond, S., et al. "Treatment of short normal children with growth hormone—a cautionary tale?" *Lancet.* 1990; 336: 1331–1334.

33. Kanaka-Gantenbein, C., Mastorakos, G., and Chrousos, G. "Endocrine-related causes and consequences of intrauterine growth retardation." *Annals of the New York Academy of Science.* 2003; 997: 150–157.

34. "How much does human growth hormone cost for children? Here's an estimate." HGH For Children, March 2, 2015. http://growthhormonenetwork.com/.

35. Rossi, W. "Commentary on treating short stature with growth hormone." *Virtual Mentor: Ethics Journal of the American Medical Association.* 2005; 7(11).

36. Nicholas, W. "Sir Francis Galton and the birth of eugenics." *Annual Review of Genetics* 2001; 35: 83–101.

37. Erling, A. "Why do some children of short stature develop psychologically well while others have problems?" *European Journal of Endocrinology.* 2004; 151: S35–S39.

38. Sandberg, D., Brook, A., and Campos, S. "Short stature: A psychosocial burden requiring growth hormone therapy?" *Pediatrics.* 1994; 94: 832–840.

39. Lee, J., et. al. "Short stature in a population-based cohort: Social, emotional, and behavioral functioning." *Pediatrics.* 2009; 124(3): 903–910.

THREE | SHORTCHANGED IN THE WORKPLACE

1. Keyes, Ralph. *The Height of Your Life.* Boston: Little, Brown, 1980.

2. Gawley, T., Perks, T., and Curtis, J. "Height, gender and authority status at work: Analyses for a national sample of Canadian workers." *Sex Roles.* 2009; 60(3): 208–222.

3. Rauch, Jonathan. "Short guys finish last." *The Economist.* December 23, 1995.

4. Schwandtner, Gerhard. "Inside the mind of H. Ross Perot." *Selling Power Magazine.* August 14, 1990.

5. Kurtz, D. "Physical appearance and stature: important variables in sales recruiting." *Personnel Journal.* 1969; 48: 981–983.

6. Hensley, W. "Height as a measure of success in academe." *Psychology: A Journal of Human Behavior.* 1993; 30(1): 40–46.

7. Gladwell, Malcolm. *Blink: The Power of Thinking without Thinking.* New York: Little, Brown, 2005.

8. Hensley, "Height as a measure of success."

9. Case, A., and Paxson, C. "Stature and status: Height, ability and labor market outcomes." *Journal of Political Economy.* 2008; 116(3): 499–532.

10. Chu, S., and Geary, K. "Physical stature influences character perception in women." *Personality and Individual Differences.* 2005; 38(8): 1927–1934.

11. Loh, E. "The economic effects of physical appearance." *Social Science Quarterly.* 1993; 74(2): 420–438.

12. Deck, L. "Buying brains by the inch." *The Journal of College and University Personnel Association.* 1968; 19: 33–37.

13. Wang, S. "Statistical Discrimination, Productivity and the Height of Immigrants." *ILR Review.* 2015; 68(3): 529–557.

14. Persico, N., Postelewaite, A., and Silverman, D. "The effect of adolescent experience on labor market outcomes: The case of height." *Journal of Political Economy* 2004; 112(5): 1019–1053.

15. Persico et al., "The effect of adolescent experience."

16. Persico et al., "The effect of adolescent experience."

17. Melamed, T., and Bozionelos, N. "Managerial promotion and height." *Psychological Reports.* 1992; 71(6): 587–593.

18. Cinnirella, F., and Winter, J. "Size matters! Body height and labor market discrimination: A cross-European analysis." Mannheim Research Institute for the Economics of Aging. Paper presented at the Cesifo Area Conference on Employment and Social Protection, May 2009.

19. Engemann, K., and Owyang, M. "So much for that merit raise: The link between wages and appearance." *The Regional Economist.* April 2005, 10–11.

20. Judge, Timothy, and Cable, Daniel. "The effect of physical height on workplace success and income: Preliminary test of a theoretical model." *Journal of Applied Psychology* 2004; 89(3): 428–441.

21. Keys, *Height of Your Life.*

22. Keys, *Height of Your Life.*

23. Cinnirella and Winter, "Size matters!"

24. Lindqvist, Eric. "Height and leadership." Research Institute of Industrial Economics (IFN), Working Paper No. 835, 2010.

25. Brown, Stephen L. "How much is income influenced by height and sex?" November 1, 2011. http://www.shortsupport.org/Research /external.html.

26. Ribaya, Rio Rose. "Russia bans gays, disabled, short people from driving." *Christian Times,* January 13, 2015.

27. "The rise of China: Employers favour recruits who stand head and shoulders above their peers." *The Economist.* October 25, 2014.

28. Rosenberg, Isaac B. "Height discrimination in employment." *Utah Law Review.* 2009; 3: 907–953.

29. 410 F. Supp. 873 (C.D. Cal 1976).

30. 56 F. 3d 934 (EE-MN-0086 D. Minn. Jan. 14, 1993).

31. 608 F. 2d 327 (9th Cir. 1979).

32. Rosenberg, "Height discrimination in employment," 907–953.

33. *McElmurry v. Arizona Dept. of Agriculture* (D. Ariz. June 11, 2013).

34. *McElmurry v. Arizona Dept. of Agriculture* (D. Ariz. May 2, 2014).

35. 29 C.F.R. § 1630 and EEOC Interpretive Manual.

36. Engemann and Owyang, "So much for that merit raise."

37. Judge, T., and Cable, D. "When it comes to pay, do the thin win? The effect of weight on pay for men and women." *Journal of Applied Psychology.* 2011 Jan; 96(1): 95–112; and Engemann, and Owyang, "So much for that merit raise."

1. Angus, D. "Height, health and development." *Proceedings of the National Academy of Sciences.* 2007 Aug; 104(33): 13232–13237.

2. Samaras, Thomas. *Human Body Size and the Laws of Scaling: Physiological, Performance, Growth, Longevity and Ecological Ramifications.* New York: Nova Science Publishers, 2007.

3. Green, J., Cairnes, B., et al. "Height and cancer incidence in the Million Women Study: Prospective cohort and meta-analysis of prospective studies of height and total cancer risk." *Lancet.* 2011; 12(8): 785–794.

4. Kabat, G., Anderson, M., et al. "Adult stature and risk of cancer at different anatomic sites in a cohort of postmenopausal women." *Cancer Epidemiology, Biomarkers & Prevention.* 2013; 22(8): OF1–OF11. http://cebp.aacrjournals.org/content/cebp/early/2013/07/25/1055 -9965.EPI-13-0305.full.pdf.

5. Samaras, T. T., et al. "Is height related to longevity?" *Life Sciences.* 2003; 72(16): 1781–1802.

6. Freedman, D., Khan, L., et al. "Relation of childhood height to obesity among adults: The Bogalusa heart study." *Pediatrics.* 2002; 109(2): 1–7.

7. Austinaras, T. T. "Are 20th century recommendations for growth and height correct? A review." *South African Journal of Clinical Nutrition.* 2009; 22(4): 171–176.

8. Stulp, Gert, and Barrett, Louise. "Evolutionary perspectives on human height variation." *Biological Reviews.* 2016; 91(1): 206–234.

9. Wiseman, Paul. "Fabric of a long life." *USA Today.* January 3, 2002.

10. "Graphic: Bodies built for soccer." *Wall Street Journal.* June 5, 2014.